P9-DCC-202

What Others Are Saying about This Book...

Returning Soldiers Speak is not only a worthy cause dedicated to those who have sacrificed immeasurably, but also an invaluable project that reveals the untold human side of the warrior mindset with brutal honesty. From Nazi Germany to modern Iraq, there's a perfect balance of bravado and self-deprecation that can only come from war veterans. The book offers immense therapeutic value for both writer and reader; a powerful collection of raw narratives that are all at once shocking, horrifying, heartbreaking, and laugh-out-loud funny. It doesn't get any more real than this.

—**Grant Murray, former counterterrorist agent,**
U.S. Department of Homeland Security

Leilani Squire has created an unusual algebra with *Returning Soldiers Speak*, an equation in which both sides of the forum benefit. The writers are able to purge these memories by "exteriorizing" them through the written word, while the audience benefits by this uniquely fresh educational insight to rare real-life experience, that in many cases may be so far outside their own as to beg belief. Sometimes the words come hard, and a writer chooses to hide behind a surrogate reader. This is understandable because, as with much confessional writing, the exposure carries an emotional price, but for that very reason, the audience knows the words are delivered straight from the heart.

—**John Rixey Moore, Ex-Special Forces Airborne Ranger,**
Actor, Award-Winning author of
Hostage of Paradox **and** *Company of Stone*

In this book, returning soldiers speak up about regret, solace, and transformation—and it is our duty to listen to what they have to say.

—**Sandra Fluck, Co-owner of Bookscover2cover**

In *Returning Soldiers Speak* readers will find dreams and nightmares, poems and memoirs, metaphysical musings and stream of consciousness therapy. The reader will also experience a remarkable balance between hope and fear, destiny and fate, and so it is to the credit of the one who compiled these stories and achieved that balance that I offer this homage.

—**Glenn Schiffman, Author of** *The Way I Was Taught*

These stories are all chapters of history. We're always so confident there will never be "another World War II," "another Vietnam," "another Iraq," but all too often history manages to loop back around and bite us in the ass. So long as there's a chance our sons or daughters or grandchildren will be called to face similar trials, I want them fortified with the testimony of veterans like these.

—**Jon Zelazny, 2LT (retired), 401ˢᵗ Civil Affairs, USAR**

This book is an awesome example of how writing one's story can begin the journey of healing. As difficult as it is for a veteran to write their story; it is so necessary that they can share their story so others will understand. It is here where the healing begins. These writings are a gift from the veterans. This gift allows us to be part of their healing journey.

—Kathy Lynch, MFT Clinical Director at
Wellness Works, Glendale, California

As a Combat Veteran Survivor of Vietnam and of long time PTSD, I applaud Ms. Squire and all of the contributing authors! It is important that these stories and others like them be shared and published because they are a cathartic form of exposure to our guarded truth and an important contribution to our post traumatic growth as individuals and as a country.

—Miguel Garbriel Vazquez, MA Psychology, and
Natural Healer/EFT Counselor and Trauma Specialist

A soldier who has been in conflict often under the most grueling conditions returns to the life he or she left behind as an altered human being. What they have witnessed or enacted in the course of military duty is often far beyond the realm of what family, friends and the larger community can comprehend. This passionate book is comprised of such accounts and impressions, the voices of veterans.

—Ric Gentry, Co-Founder Returning Soldiers Speak

What a moving and important book! In this astounding collection we hear the voices of veterans of many different wars. Listening to what they have to say can bring us all closer to appreciating the innate desire for peace in our hearts whether our battles are visible and external or within us.

—Gail Soffer, Development and Marketing Director,
Wellness Works

Returning Soldiers Speak

An Anthology of
Prose and Poetry

by Soldiers and Veterans

Compiled by Leilani Squire

BETTIE YOUNGS BOOKS

Copyright © 2014, Leilani Squire

All rights reserved, including the right to reproduce this work in any form whatsoever, without permission in writing from the publisher, except for brief passages in connection with a review.

Disclaimer: All entries in this book represent the individual author's experience.

We are grateful for permission to use the following entrees:
"Kentucky Clouds Over the Green-Eyed Monster" which first appeared in *Tygerburning, New England College* and "Intravenous" first appeared in *The Iowa Review.* Reprinted with permission by Hugh Martin.

"Hostage of Paradox, Chapter 23" Copyright ©2012 by John Rixey Moore, published by Bettie Youngs Books. Reprinted with permission from the Publisher.

"But You Made the Front Page!" an excerpt from Chapter 6 of "But You Made the Front Page!" Copyright © 2012 by Sonny Fox, and distributed by Argo Navis. Reprinted with permission of the Carol Mann Agency and Sonny Fox.

Cover design by Min Gates
Interior design by Min Gates
Senior editor and compiler, Leilani Squire
Line editing by Jazmin Gomez
Logo by Timothy Grant

BETTIE YOUNGS BOOK PUBLISHERS
www.BettieYoungsBooks.com
Info@BettieYoungsBooks.com

If you are unable to order this book from your local bookseller or online from Amazon or Barnes & Noble, or from Espresso or Read How You Want, you may order directly from the publisher (info@BettieYoungsBooks.com).

1. Squire, Leilani. 2. Military Experiences. 3. Bettie Youngs Books. 4. Soldiers. 5. Veterans. 6. Vietnam War. 7. Iraq War. 8. Persian Gulf War. 9. Desert Storm. 10. World War II. 11. Military Sexual Trauma-MST. 12. Post Traumatic Stress Disorder. 13. Veterans Issues.

Book ISBN: 978-1-936332-62-5
eBook ISBN: 978-1-936332-63-2

Printed in the United States of America

Dedication

Dedicated to the men and women who have worn or wear
the uniform of the Military

….and

In remembrance of Lee Mingh Sloca

Table of Contents

Acknowledgements

Lee Mingh Sloca was the first to talk to me about putting on a program with Returning Soldiers, but his sudden and untimely death stopped that project before we could finish. So I decided to continue in Lee's memory and renamed it *Returning Soldiers Speak*. Even though his vision has morphed into another vision, the groundwork came from his initial idea. I am forever grateful for Lee's friendship, poetry, passion, and love of life. It was an honor to know him and to call him my best friend.

All the soldiers and veterans who contributed to this anthology and who have participated in my creative writing workshops at the Greater Los Angeles Veterans Hospital and Wellness Works hold a special place in my heart. You are my teachers! Your courage and honesty, integrity and sense of duty and pride are a constant inspiration to me. Your stories make me want to do my best. My appreciation for you is boundless.

I humbly and lovingly say thank you to my sisters, Jeannie, Sandy and Kathy, for their encouragement and belief in this project. And to my dear friend, Glenn Schiffman, a really big thank you for your encouragement when I needed it most and proofreading the entire manuscript when I needed that the most. You are a true friend.

I am especially grateful to Eric Maisel for his poignant Foreword and his continual wisdom and support, and to Bill Mann who tells it like it is, which leads always to authentic work, of which this book is a part.

A special thank you for your amazing proofreading and friendship: Gedda Ilves, Annette Robinson, Richard Fluck and the Studio City Writers Group—you stepped up to the plate when I really needed you. Thank you to Ric Gentry, David Obsusin, Kathy Lynch, Grant Murray, Jon Zelazny, Cheryl Montelle, Gail Soffer, and Miguel Gabriel Vazquez.

An extra special thanks to my publisher Bettie Youngs Books for without Bettie Youngs this book would not be what it is. Bettie understands just how important it is for soldiers and veterans to tell their stories. She has my deep appreciation and respect. And to John Rixey Moore for introducing me to Bettie. I am also grateful to her talented staff in the preparation of this book.

The list could go on and on. But I will end with the biggest thank to my husband, Charles Smallwood, who believes in me like none other. So many times he has said, "You can do it. This book is important." Thank you, my dear husband.

John Rixey Moore

Introduction

My father served thirty years in the U.S. Navy. He was deployed to Okinawa and his job was to maintain and catapult jets on an aircraft carrier's deck when I was born. That was during the Korean War. My father didn't talk about the Korean War, even when I asked him about it as an adult. What did he see? What did he know that he kept hidden inside? Why wouldn't he tell me? What stopped him from talking? I'll never know what he experienced and this haunts me.

I don't want our young men and women who are coming back from Iraq and Afghanistan to be like my father: silent and hidden. I don't want the veterans of Vietnam to be pushed to the side, alienated and forgotten. I don't want the soldiers of the Korean War—or any war—to suffer alone. I don't want those who have suffered or are suffering from Military Sexual Trauma (MST), Traumatic Brain Injury (TBI), homelessness, joblessness, addictions to drugs and alcohol to be in pain, isolated from the rest of society.

The soldiers and veterans whose writing appears in this book are the most courageous people I know. To write what they have written was not an easy task and, perhaps, one of the most difficult things they have done. It may sound odd to say that, knowing what they have experienced and endured while serving their country. But it takes courage, honesty and authenticity to bare one's heart and soul on the page so others may listen. They have done just that.

Returning Soldiers Speak comprises the nitty-gritty stories of those who have served in the U.S. Military. In order to retain the authenticity of the veteran's voice not many editorial changes have been made. To change a slight variance in tone or grammar would change the lilt in the voice of the narrator, a nuance in the story.

—Leilani Squire, Los Angeles, October, 2013

Foreword

As a young man I was both a soldier (1965-1968) and, after mustering out of the Army, an anti-war activist. That is neither a paradox nor an example of growth. I was both things all along: a young man with all of a young man's needs and desires, including the need to test himself, a hunger for adventure, and, yes, even an acute desire to march; and a thinking person completely suspicious of patriotic slogans and the motivations and intentions of politicians.

Each man and woman represented in this volume is his or her own confusing and complicated mix of contradictions. One rebels at every turn while serving and then is devastated to be discharged and not allowed to join his buddies in Iraq. Another feels ruined by his combat experiences, completely emotionally adrift, and yet feels compelled to announce that his military service taught him important lessons about discipline and duty. This, and not an easy word like "hero," is reality.

We do not tend to like the truth; and veterans, knowing this as keenly as anyone else, have historically not spoken their truth. They have felt obliged to play along, as if the only way to manifest honor was to fall silent about their feelings and deny their experiences. This book, then, is an exception: a bit of truth-telling in a sea of flag-waving, on the one hand, and scorn, on the other.

Its main virtue may be the extent to which the veterans themselves were healed, or partially healed, by speaking. But maybe you will be moved, too; and arrive at a clearer picture of what it is really like to serve and to kill. It is odd to say that I hope that you will also find some joy in all this. Yet I think you will. Writing does not turn a horror into a tea party but there is more than spilled blood in these pages: there is also something about the human heart. —Eric Maisel

Eric Maisel, PhD, the author of forty books, is a columnist for *Professional Artist* magazine and a featured blogger for *Psychology Today*

1

an excellent sunday dinner...
by Burk Wiedner

"Is that a grave?" I asked when I saw Dad digging in back of the garden. I remembered our little brother being buried the year before.

The Greek Chorus sang softly, the sound coming as though from far away:

"The world has not yet come into focus for this boy."

Dad told me that this was to become a special shelter: "Just in case of an emergency, you know?"

"Can't we just stay in the basement when the planes come?"

Dad did not answer. He was hard at work again, not hearing my question. But I, watching as he shoveled spade after spade of earth out of the hollow, knew that my friends and I could make this bunker into a lair of our own.

Dad's shirtsleeves were rolled up above the elbows and I saw his glasses fog up, sweat gathering on his face. It looked as though he was about to finish the job. But suddenly lightning and thunder preceded a cloudburst.

It is 1943, and I am Burckhardt, the eight-year-old middle child of Otto and Hildegard Wiedner. My brother Wolfgang is four years older and my sister Marianne two years younger. My parents built our house a long time ago, in *Kleinmachnow* just off the southwestern border of Berlin, Germany— even before Wolfgang was born. Our street is typical of the residential areas of the town. None of the houses look alike. The street surfaces consist of uneven, rounded cobbles, and even the sidewalks are made of smaller stones, smooth at the top. There is a row of small trees hugging the curb where we

1

live at 3 *Eichenweg* (Oak Way), but there are no oaks on this street, except one at the corner.

In the summer, light streams into our sunroom. During the winter, it can be shut off from the living room behind by a roll-up partition. Dad's study next door houses the telephone and our wood-clad radio, the latter with names of far-away cities on its scale. Most importantly though is the revolver in the cabinet. I am allowed to inspect it through the glass, but forbidden to touch it—or even open the door.

Opposite the hall are the stairs leading to the upper floor. They are dark, narrow and steep.

There is open land on the side toward Berlin, with a view across a thicket of small trees and bushes. From our bedroom window I have seen the glow of fire from there after the night raids, because we are at war.

In front of the house a hedge along the street has grown tall. A mature birch tree guards the gate, but Dad said it would still grow taller. In back of the house, a garden with a variety of trees provides room to roam and shade on hot days. A couple of times a month Dad mows the grass, each time making me stand back at a safe distance. I like to watch him work as he makes wide and sweeping half-circles with his scythe.

Last year when Mom brought home a new baby, a nanny named Rosel came to us. From the start I liked the sixteen-year-old serving her one-year commitment. Her face and brown eyes under black hair made her look friendly, and I accepted her as part of the family. She slept in the small bedroom, and the children—meaning us—shared another. Mom and Dad had the room behind the balcony, above the sunroom.

I never knew that Rosel's father was Jewish. Even if the adults had talked about those things it would not have mattered. The only thing I knew about Jewish people was that when they dropped a fork or spoon at the table they were not allowed to finish their meal. But I don't know if Rosel had ever dropped a utensil.

On a summer Sunday that year Uncle Walter, a colleague from the school for deaf and mute children where Dad works, came to help with the shelter. Mother told me that he was very sad, because he had just come back from Hamburg where the funeral of his daughter-in-law and grandchild had been held. His son Helmut had been present, on bereavement leave, from the Russian front.

After air raids early in the war I did hear about people dying in Hamburg. But I was not concerned, because only the adults had information about those kinds of things. I had heard that it was a long way from Berlin, and the raids here had not harmed us anyway.

But the Greek Chorus understood, and chanted:

an excellent sunday dinner... by Burk Wiedner

"In Hamburg ... two-thousand-pound bombs filled with high-explosives crushed attics, floors and pulverized roofs so that phosphorous fire bombs could then enter lower floors to incinerate and reduce to ashes all that was left to burn. Within minutes the fire rose high into the air, creating hurricane-force winds and flinging entire roof sections about like kindling wood. Asphalt, melted in the streets as bubbling lava, incinerated those who had fled their basements in terror."

The family of Walter Knuth's son had died there during one of those raids. I felt sorry for Uncle Walter.

The bunker being readied in the back had been an object of deep interest to me since Dad first started digging. That weekend he and his friend were both working in that corner of the garden surrounded by small trees and bushes. A sandy patch, intended as a play area for us, was left there when the house was built. The lair would be better still.

So I kept a sharp lookout on their progress. Both men worked as if they were having a good time. They were talking, too, but I couldn't really make out what was said. One time I saw Uncle Walter standing with his back against the wall and rubbing his temples with both hands, while Dad thoughtfully scraped a few pebbles off the side of the excavation with his spade. It made a rasping sound. But when I approached they always stopped talking, and returned to their task with renewed vigor. Finally, Dad came out of the hole and sat on the sand with his back to me as I went to inspect their work.

"I hung up," I heard Dad say. "I didn't ask questions! And I haven't heard from either David or his family since!" He seemed upset.

"Who did you call, Dad, and why did you hang up?" I asked.

Dad looked around and stood up, a strange expression appearing on his face.

"You don't know the person, Burckhardt. How long have you been standing there?"

Why did he look so worried? I told him that I had just walked up, and then watched him hurry down the short ladder. I thought it strange that he moved as quickly as that when he had rested so peacefully a minute earlier. Yet now both resumed their labor energetically, and I went to tease the neighbor's dog barking at me behind the fence.

At lunchtime, after we had all eaten spaghetti and tomato sauce on the patio, my dad and his friend disappeared into Dad's study. I checked their project one more time before reluctantly taking my homework into the living room to get ready for the coming week. They left the frosted glass door leading into the adjacent den partially open, and I heard Uncle Walter's voice coming through.

He said something about 'horror' and, understanding the word; I wondered what he was referring to.

"Well, you know that there were signs since 1938, and even earlier than that..." Dad replied, his voice trailing off. Silence followed, with me sitting very still so as not to be heard.

What horror, I wondered? I knew of no horror.

Then I heard Dad's voice again: "Back then I gave private lessons to the deaf and mute son of David Schapskie in *Dahlem*, and we soon became fast friends. David had been an officer in WWI just as you and I, and he owned a large factory in *Zehlendorf*. He was as good a German as anyone I know and, uh... was also a Jew. We often talked about the National Socialists, and he knew that I had joined the party."

I could not quite understand what Uncle Walter said next, but thought that he asked once again how all this could have happened. "And why in God's name did we join up?" he then added.

"Well, in 1935, just before you came into the school, we were told that the principal of each school had to join the party." Dad did not need to identify 'the party' as even I knew there was only one.

"Lehmann put in his application, but he was rejected for his former membership in the Freemasons," Dad continued. "Eventually they came to me as the vice-principal. I told them that I was not a joiner and did not want to become politically involved. It was not a smart thing to say, and after more give and take I signed up."

I heard nothing for a while and, not knowing why they were talking about the party, thought that they had finished. But I was wrong.

"It was not wise to resist. The wife and children..." Dad spoke up, and fell silent again. Then he cleared his throat.

What was there to resist? Being a member of the party meant to support the *Reich*. It was a good thing. I was sure of that.

I felt the urge to sneeze and fought hard against the impulse. Fortunately, it went away.

"And what about David?" I heard Uncle Walter ask.

"My youngest, Marianne, had her first birthday on November 9th in 1938, and we had a few people here to celebrate her big day." Dad's voice sounded strangely coarse. There was a pause, but he went on once more. "Suddenly, a neighbor stormed in and said that a German-Jewish exchange student had murdered a German Embassy employee in Paris. Some of us came in here and listened as Goebbels predicted action against the Jews in a short speech on the radio."

"I listened to it as well," I heard Uncle Walter say.

"The next morning I saw the burnt-out shell of the Synagogue on *Fasa-*

nenstrasse on my way to work," Dad continued. "In the afternoon I called David but there was no answer. I tried the following day, and again no one picked up. And when I called one more time from school on the day I was to give the lesson to his son, a stranger's voice answered."

There was another spell of silence in the next room.

"That's when I hung up. I told you! I hung up." It was Dad's voice again. "I said nothing and asked no questions! And I have not seen or heard from David for these past five years!"

Dad's voice became progressively louder, but now there was only the sound of papers being shifted around—nothing more. This, I realized, was what he had said when I walked over to watch them digging. But it did not make any sense. What was the horror? They had talked about nothing horrible. And now, having listened the way I did, I could not even ask.

Once again the Greek Chorus had the answer, but sang it outside my hearing:

"All are weak hearted and terrified. One word can undo a family. Everyone looks upon any stranger as an informer."

"Come on. Let's go out and dig some more," Uncle Walter said after several minutes had passed. The door to the hallway was open and I saw them walk past it. Uncle Walter's hand rested on Dad's shoulder.

Later that afternoon in the sunroom we had juice and cookies Mom had baked while the men drank *Ersatz Kaffee*. I heard that it is not real coffee but they drank it anyway. Then I watched them smoke their pipes, and I took in the aroma of the tobacco. It was comforting as always.

Finally, we said good-bye to our visitor. Mother gave him a hug and kiss before he left.

"I wish we could do something for Walter and Ella, and for Helmut," Mom said.

I knew she liked them, even though they were Dad's age. He was fifty-eight. I couldn't imagine someone having a friend twenty years older, but I liked Auntie Ella and Uncle Walter too. I remembered our little brother Bernfried dying and concluded that was for Mother like the loss of a grandchild in Hamburg was for them.

Because of all that was going on, it was not strange to feel pride to be a *Friedenskind* (peace child). My brother and sister, as well as I, were all born before the outbreak of war. I had heard that one could buy anything then, even chocolate and oranges, and no one had to go to the basement when planes came overhead.

A long time ago, I remember a giant *Zeppelin* (dirigible) flying low over our main boulevard, and I watched until it disappeared behind the trees. I was quite certain that having been born into such a world clothed us with a special status. And there was other corroboration, as I understood it. Mother brought home the little baby, and he was not a peace child—even though Bernfried means 'Bern's Peace.' He died just days after he had come to us. It made me sad because that was only the second time that I saw Mom cry. Dad mentioned in passing that Mother was awarded a medal from the government on the occasion of her fourth child, but she never talked about it.

I still could remember the day when Mom cried for the first time. She didn't want to let us see it, turning away while we were in the living room. When she wiped her eyes I knew it. I went around to face her, and there were tears.

"Are you crying, Mom?" I asked with watering eyes, knowing the answer ahead of time.

"No, no, it's all right," she said, trying to suppress her sobs, and ran out to the kitchen.

It was because war had broken out. I heard it first from Dad. Later the teacher said in class that Poland had fired shells into our country, attacking a bank, and we had to defend ourselves. It made me want to be old enough to fight.

Except for school my life was good, and I didn't reckon war would or even could change that. As Dad taught deaf and mute children in Berlin he usually came home early in the afternoon, barring unforeseen circumstances. He was not in this war because he had fought in the *Great War* both in Russia and France. That war is now called WWI. I had been told that when he had come home after WWI his first wife died and he eventually married our mother. He told me that he was too old to go back into the military now, but he did not seem that old to me. I was glad that he could stay with us though.

I knew that Dad had been a great soldier and I would be as well. He had taken the revolver in his study from one of the three soldiers he captured in Russia, and his Iron Cross was in a drawer of his desk. He hardly ever talked about those things unless I asked, and even then I never found out much.

At times I went into the attic to look at his old dress uniform stored there in a box. The attic is unfinished and the wood creaks when I go up the steps. I could always hear the wind or, on rainy days, the raindrops beating down on the roof when climbing the stairs. The tunic of Dad's uniform felt stiff and dusty. It had two rows of golden buttons, with a ribbon on the left side. I was not allowed to touch the saber but liked the dark-blue helmet with the golden spike. When I put it on it covered my eyes and smelled vinegary like old food. The uniforms were different then, not like the ones I will wear when I grow up. Today I asked Dad once more about the war.

"How many people did you kill in the war, Dad?"

"You don't want to kill anyone, Burckhardt," he responded quietly. "Life is very precious and when someone is killed his family will miss him forever."

"Yes, but did you kill anyone?"

"As an officer you rarely fire a rifle. I was always thankful for that."

It looked as though I would not get anywhere this time either. But he continued.

"War is an awful experience. This one will be over before you grow up. Now get ready to do your school work."

Reference to homework meant that the conversation was over for sure.

Recently, Rosel acquired a friend. A few weeks into the affair, when we were already in bed, there was loud crying and stamping of feet outside our room. Dad had forbidden Rosel to spend time with the friend. I needed to know what was going on and Wolfgang, more knowledgeable in the way of worldly affairs than I, explained that her friend was a boy. It grated on me that he always had more information, but as this news held no importance I went to sleep.

That night the air raid sirens wailed and we were told to get dressed quickly. I recognized the sound of the siren even before I woke up, as if I had been waiting for it. Dad opened all windows in the house after lights had been turned off and we rushed into the basement to sit in the narrow hallway. Mother closed the doors to the three rooms that served mostly as storage areas and held the central heating system. As we waited for the sounds of the *flak* (anti-aircraft guns) and droning of heavy engines above, I shivered slightly. It was not cold and, in fact, I felt hot. There was one window at the end of the hall, below ground level, but it was of course covered with cloth as all the others, and blocked any view of what we might otherwise have seen in the night sky.

"Why do we always have to open the windows upstairs, Dad?" I asked. It seemed a waste of time.

"Nearby explosions would break the glass if the windows are closed," he answered. It did not make sense, but I accepted his explanation. It was a good thing that only the windows would break. And all three adults—I had accepted Rosel as a person with authority—looked calm.

I listened for the whistling of falling bombs while the planes passed overhead, having been told that if one hears the whistling noise of a bomb it would not be a direct hit. Explosions sounded like distant drum rolls and now I watched Wolfgang to see if I should be afraid. He did not look worried. Nothing was going to happen.

After the all clear it was good to feel the warmth of the bed. Over the weekend Wolfgang and I would go on a shrapnel search. Marianne was not interested in shrapnel and I knew that she would not come along. I hoped to find bigger and better shrapnel than my brother, and would go alone if I had to.

At times, Mother took me to some stores not far from home. Meat was available at the butcher shop if we had not exceeded the limits of our ration cards, and the bakery was in *Stahnsdorf* via a short bus ride. One Saturday morning Mom asked me to go there and buy *broetchen*—breakfast rolls. I was stunned. I wanted to ride the bus on my own but was not sure that she would let me.

"Me?" I asked cautiously, trying to carry an air of confidence in my voice.

"Yes, of course," she responded reassuringly, smiling at me. "Do you know how to get there, Burckhardt?"

We had friends living a block from the bakery, and had often visited them. Besides, having been quizzed repeatedly on those matters, I could recite my parents' names, and knew our address and phone number.

After being tested once again on the route and armed with money and ration cards I was on my way. Three blocks from home I climbed the stairs of the yellow double-decker bus, feeling the eyes of the conductor on me as I went. The movement of the bus felt rocky and the steps were steep, but I wanted him to know that this eight-year-old had handled many such trips before. I held onto the rail tightly as the vehicle gathered speed. Once seated in the front row where you can see the bus turn into corners, the familiar row houses and shops plunged by as I watched the branches of trees sweeping close to hitting the windows, just inches from my face.

Passing a group of workers along the way performing street maintenance under the watchful eyes of a uniformed guard, I wondered why they weren't at war. When I had asked Dad once before he had been of little help, only speculating that they might be prisoners from the local jail. The bus moved on and soon reached its final stop where the bakery was located. I felt confident as I ordered the rolls, and put them into a small net given me for that purpose. The return trip was easy, and I had proven myself a man.

Life has not always been a success story for me, however. We ate our dinner in the early afternoon, and typically had sandwiches in the evening. That was my favorite meal, but I had decided to hate *quark*, a form of slimy cottage cheese. One evening Mother handed me a slice of bread with margarine and *quark* piled on top of it. She knew I wouldn't eat it. Refusing to touch it, I was soon screaming at the top of my voice—taking care not to open the mouth wide enough to have the food stuffed into it. There was food here I liked better. I continued my protest until Dad, appearing calm as always, told me that I would be grounded for the weekend. I ate, but it tasted as gooey as I knew it would.

"I don't know why he makes such a racket," Wolfgang said. "It's good *quark.*"

He looked at me like a teacher. I didn't need another teacher. There were too many of them already, and it made me mad. Because I was already in trouble I remained quiet, chewing my sandwich like a cow. It took a long time to get it down.

It had not been two nights since the last air raid when sirens wailed again at night, sending the adults into the same hectic dance of shutting off lights and opening windows while we dressed. But tonight we were going to join the neighbors in their basement. I rode over on Dad's shoulders while Marianne was with Mom; Wolfgang walked ahead with Rosel. I strained to identify the engine sounds of incoming aircraft but on this short walk heard nothing. Not a single light was visible except for the moon peering through clouds and branches of the birch at our gate. To my right some of the wet cobbles glistened in the dark as we passed. I could feel the cold of the night and a few drops of water falling from the tree.

Mother had made arrangements with our two women neighbors for all of us to stay together during future raids. Lotte Mueller whom we called Auntie Mueller and her sister, Auntie Berg—the latter as tall as her sibling was short—had lived together since Mueller's husband, a set designer at the Berlin Opera House, died. I heard that Auntie Berg had never been married. Sometimes they called me into their house and gave me cookies.

This time, in their basement, only I was handed a real steel helmet. I wore it from then on during all of our nocturnal visits. There were no helmets for Wolfgang and Marianne. My liner fit and it made me feel better: I liked the scent of the leather around my head and felt like a soldier. And this basement was nicer than our own cellar; more of a sitting room somewhere upstairs, and here it was easier for me to look like I wasn't afraid.

They also had some comfortable chairs and end tables, and I listened to the adults talking about the purchase of emergency rations while my head was anchored in the steel pot. Presently, explosions outside were easily identified as *flak.*

Following the all clear—a steady note of the sirens lasting a minute or longer—now back in the bedroom looking into Berlin through the window—an orange glow illuminated the sky. The window would remain open, and I listened for the sound of airplane engines. I pulled the cover over my ears but could still hear Wolfgang and Marianne breathe in the dark. They too were awake, but no one spoke.

I like to sleep on my side with an arm under my head and the feather bed tucked between my knees, but had come to believe that it brought on air raids, and I had given it up. Now that we had had several raids over a short time I went back to sleep the way I liked.

In the morning Mother told me that I had to come down for breakfast. *"Wach auf,"* she said, gently touching my shoulder. "Wake up. It's time to get ready."

I considered the possibility of playing sick but knew it wouldn't work. Wolfgang was already in the bathroom, and Marianne had gotten dressed. The windows were closed now, and I slowly slipped the feather bed back to test the air.

To the three of us on our way to school that morning, the neighborhood looked normal, with birds in the trees and a dog barking nearby. Not really knowing why, I imagined that we were still living in peace, but I would have preferred to be a soldier fighting in heroic battles.

Every day, before classes could start, we had to line up in formation in the school yard to sing the National Anthem and the *Horst-Wessel Song.* I liked the words but hated standing at attention with my arm extended in the Nazi salute. My motive for disliking this ritual was not political; I was interested in anything military, but it hurt to keep the arm raised for all that time. I always stood in the second or third row. It was better when I was behind another student and could rest my arm on his shoulder. I didn't like school, but this is part of what I will have to do as a soldier when I grow up. Our teacher had told us that refusing to give the salute is a serious crime, but I didn't mind it anyway.

I wanted to be a soldier; time did not seem to move quickly enough. Wolfgang already had a uniform, and each time I saw him in it my heart beat faster as envy overcame me. He was a member of the *Jungvolk,* also called *Pimpfe* ("tykes"), an organization created by the government to prepare boys for entry into the *Hitler Youth* at age fourteen.

"What is it like?" I asked him.

"It's good."

That Wolfgang found it good made it even worse for me.

"Why?"

"I like it." He fell silent for a few seconds, but then added: "And sometimes I don't like it."

"Why?"

"Don't know. Probably because there will be more in the *Hitler Youths."*

I didn't understand, but decided not to seek clarification. It was better if he thought that I had understood.

But now even him wearing that new uniform was a mere irritation. A new development was bigger than anything that had ever happened! Wolfgang announced that he would go to *Krinica,* Poland, for several weeks.

Every one of the boys was going! I had heard Dad talk to him about it, and so it had to be true.

"You want to see where *Krinica* is?" Wolfgang asked Marianne and me, poring over an atlas. I almost said no but needed to look at where he was pointing to on the map. The name was written in such tiny letters that I could hardly make it out.

"It's a small place," I said to my sister.

"We'll have maneuvers there. We might even have rifles." Wolfgang sounded matter-of-fact. In addition to what he could look forward to, it was his calm fortitude that irritated me so.

On the day of his departure Mom, Marianne and I went to *Anhalter Bahnhof* to see him off. I could only stare with wonder at the boys hanging out of the train windows. I wanted for my time to come, and to be someone like that. Why could I not play war games and even learn to shoot a rifle as well as they? And now Wolfgang was going to Poland, a country I could only dream about. That, too, was possible only for my big brother.

It was then that the Greek Chorus rendered one more song:

"In 1943, Johann Paul Kremer, MD, a German SS lieutenant assigned to a concentration camp in Poland not far from Krinica, is keeping a diary. On September 6, Doctor Kremer's entry reads: today an excellent Sunday dinner; tomato soup, a half chicken with potatoes and red cabbage (20 gr fat), dessert and magnificent vanilla ice cream."

The chorus paused for a moment, as if to make sure that I was paying attention, and concluded:

"The camp is called Auschwitz-Birkenau."

It broke my heart.

WW II

2

But You Made the Front Page!
by Sonny Fox

As we got into the second week of December, we noticed a rise in the clatter of equipment and tanks coming from the German positions across the river. After a couple of nights of this I reported it to the Captain. His orders instructed him to double our patrols. Since we were a mile or more away from the next position north of us, that meant loading into a jeep in the middle of the cold December night and, without lights, driving to a midway point between our company and the adjoining one. Not only was it freezing, but we understood the only way we would discover our lines being infiltrated was when they started shooting at us.

My other concern was the report that on occasion, the Germans had infiltrated and strung piano wire tautly across the road at about neck level. That meant if you were sitting in the front seat and ran into one of these you had a good chance of being neatly decapitated. When I had that position in the jeep, I carefully fixed my bayonet on my MI rifle with the sharp edge facing front, and made sure my head was not above the blade of the bayonet.

Although nothing happened on our two weeks of increased patrols, the grinding noise was getting more ominous. What we were hearing was Field Marshall Von Rundstedt positioning his panzer divisions and all the manpower that could be found for one last gamble by the Reich—a push out of the Ardennes through our lines and on to Antwerp.

He had chosen his attack point wisely. First the cover of the Ardennes kept his concentrations from being spotted. The front along which he decided to attack was held by two divisions. On the South was the 28th, on the North the 106th, a division that had just arrived on the front. It had never been in battle and was totally unready for this level of assault. We were dispersed along a large front with huge gaps between our positions. Although we had been sending our warnings for two weeks about the increased level of activity, back at SHAEF HQ they apparently did not believe the Germans were capable of such an offensive maneuver.

On the morning of December 16, 1944, I was awakened at 5:20 AM by artillery screeching over the farmhouse. I ran to the foxhole a few yards from the building and jumped in to find my sentries.

"How long has this been going on?"

"About 20 minutes."

I started back to the house to get the rest of my squad out. As I got close to the door, I heard an incoming and dove under the butcher block alongside the entrance. The shell passed over and I started to extricate myself but could not get free. The battle was beginning and I was stuck under a butcher block! I started to giggle. All hell was breaking loose and I was going to end my life stuck under a goddam butcher block.

I finally broke loose and dashed into the house to find my mighty band of warriors cowering in the potato cellar. I shouted them out of there and into our prepared positions on both sides of the farmhouse. Unfortunately, that meant I was out of contact with those on the far side of the building. I was with two of my squad, the others were scattered about.

At 5:30 AM, the artillery barrage lifted and green signal lights arched into the sky. The attack was officially on. Since our position was in front of the town, about 500 yards closer to the German lines, I am not sure they knew we were there. At any rate, we were able to fire at their troops without any coordinated response from them. At one point, I heard some Germans walking down the road just on the other side of the hedge that separated us from that road. As they approached our position, I pulled the pin from a grenade. I rose up enough to catch a glimpse of three soldiers chatting as they walked, as though they were on a stroll down the Unter Den Linden. I tossed the grenade and watched long enough to register their startled reaction. Then, I slid back into the foxhole to avoid the explosion.

It is amazing what I was able to see in those seconds. After one pulls the pin on a grenade and releases the lever, there is a pause of 4.5 seconds before it explodes. Perhaps, I had three seconds to scan the scene. I am sure I am remembering all of this as it happened. One of the men was wearing a Red Cross armband. I did not know that prior to tossing the grenade. If I had the time, would I have tossed the grenade far enough away so they would not have been harmed? The soldier wearing the Red Cross armband had on dark rimmed glasses and he was young. They were all young, perhaps my age—19. At the moment of their death, they might have been talking to each other about their girlfriends or their schools. They seemed not to understand they were in the middle of a war and there was a battle going on. All of this

I saw in those three seconds. All of this I remember 66 years later. What if I had decided to confront them with my rifle and they surrendered to me? I would have had to keep them in our emplacement, along with my two members of my squad, for several hours. Could I have gotten to know them as we awaited our uncertain outcome?

The vividness of that close encounter did change my feelings about the nature of war. More than the husks of burned out buildings, or graphic pictures of soldiers strewn about a battlefields, it was seeing these three young men, just feet from me, alive with energy and enjoying each other's company. Then, in a flash, they were no longer alive. I believe it is that instantaneous transformation, playing out as it did, that has kept those images alive today.

It was a long morning and it became afternoon. I had no way of contacting our HQ in town. I had no way of knowing how the rest of my squad members were doing in their emplacements on the other side of the farmhouse—facing German lines.

We were very alone.

About three o'clock in the afternoon I heard the creaking roar of tanks coming up the road toward us from the direction of Hosingen. I had no idea whose tanks were making their way toward us. It was very tense until the turret came into view and I saw it was two of our Sherman tanks. The tankers told me they had been dispatched from reserves and had been "shooting Jerries" all the way in. That meant the Germans were behind our lines. I checked and was relieved that none of my men had suffered casualties. The tankers told me they had been assigned to re-establish contact with my position and they were now under my command. Irwin, the kid from Brooklyn, now had infantry and armor under his command!

After positioning my small army, I walked back to town and dropped in on Captain Friker to find out about our grand victory. He informed me that the Germans had reached our battalion and overrun it. That would be several miles behind us. Clearly, the battle had not gone as I had supposed. I was to return to my outpost and was to be reinforced by a ranger squad. (Ranger squads were much like today's black berets—an elite fighting unit.)

So now I had my squad, the ranger squad and two tanks. While I waited to be promoted to Field Marshal, I also had to figure out how to hold onto what was becoming an increasingly exposed position. Most of the fighting in the next twelve hours was sporadic and centered in the town. The next morning, December 17, we were taking some sniper fire, but most of the fighting was taking place in the town itself. I was standing near one of our tanks, directing some suppressing fire in front of us when two tanks appeared on the horizon on the ridgeline leading into Hosingen.

"Ours or theirs?" I asked.

The tanker had his field glasses pinned to his eyes.

"Square fenders. Theirs."

As this dialogue was occurring, the turret of one of the German tanks tracked until the Panzer's 88 was aimed squarely at us, and the tank fired a round. It was right on. It hit the turret of the tank behind me but glanced off and exploded about 100 feet away. Had it hit the rounded surface squarely, you would have been spared this story. That shot was the end of the shortest tank battle in WWII. The Sherman tanks had 75MM low trajectory cannon, the Tiger tanks had high trajectory 88MM cannon. Our tanks were outgunned and they knew it. The American tank commander buttoned his turret, put the tank in gear, backed into the kitchen of the farmhouse and roared off. Our other tank, having heard from the first tank, also performed the time-honored maneuver known as, "Let's Get the Hell Out of Here."

One tank going at full speed makes a mighty noise. Two tanks raise the decibel level to a painful crescendo. As these two tanks roared off, I ran after them, yelling, "Come back. Come back," surely one of the most poignant and futile gestures of WWII. I suddenly felt VERY naked in that position.

I dispatched one of the men with a message to the Captain saying that if I did not hear to the contrary, I was going to pull my squads back into the town to join the rest of the company. By three o'clock, not having heard anything, and not being sure my messenger had even gotten through, I started sending the soldiers on a run through a cemetery, at odd intervals back into Hosingen. Only one man got creased in the abdomen, the rest made it okay.

This time my audience with Captain Friker was even more somber. Regimental was gone, about fifteen miles behind us, and divisional had signed off saying, "Good luck." Although we had held our position, the Germans had kept going behind us. Now we were thirty-five miles behind German lines. We hadn't moved. They had. We had no hope of any reinforcements arriving and no air support. My squad was assigned to occupy and hold one of the few buildings in the center of town that we still controlled. All through the night our perimeter kept shrinking. It was a surreal night of burning buildings and tanks clanking and sporadic outbursts of gunfire. And I kept dropping off to sleep. I could not help it. The next morning the Captain decided that we had no alternative but to surrender, a decision that seemed very sensible to me at the time. We were down to a handful of houses we'd held on to as long as we could.

We surrendered to the Germans at 11:00 AM on December 18, 1944. We walked out of the few houses we had left in the town. We hadn't taken many casualties in our own unit and had destroyed our jeeps and our weapons. Out we came, with our hands raised high. My emotions were wildly mixed. Relief at being alive, fear of what was about to befall us, but also a keen curiosity about what this new experience would be like. I was curious to walk through the looking glass and see the German side of the war. I think my concerns were mitigated by being part of an organized surrender. I was still with my unit. I was still an American soldier. The scene just beyond our houses underscored the wisdom to the Captain's decision. The Germans had brought up tanks and artillery, and they were all aimed at the few houses we had been holding. They were about to level us.

That day we were walked back toward the original German lines—the Aare River, the border between Luxembourg and Germany. We had to go past the position we had held when the attack started. As we were marching under guard by the Germans, one of the men in my squad piped up in a fairly loud voice, "Jeez, we got a lot of 'em, didn't we?" He may not have gotten a Purple Heart for those shins that I kicked, but I kicked him hard enough so that he should've. The Germans kept us marching through the afternoon. We found more and more of our division assembling. As it turns out, the Germans got their first big bag of American POWs in the opening days of what was to become known as The Battle of the Bulge. At seven thousand, five hundred men, it was the largest mass surrender in the entire war.

3

Hostage of Paradox
by John Rixey Moore

Shortly after my patrol with the major, team Anaconda was sent out again. This was to be another interdiction mission, slightly north of the dreaded tri-border area where one of our teams had recently been sacrificed to an operation initially assigned to me. It wasn't to be in the same region but close enough to crowd everything else from my consciousness.

A recent battalion-size engagement with the NVA had resulted in the loss of a man with a Starlight night vision scope, and the Americans had withdrawn under fire without being able to retrieve the body or the scope. Since an air strike had been called in to finish the NVA, it was hoped the remains had been destroyed along with the scope, but they wanted to be sure. The important thing was to retrieve the scope, or whatever might be left of it, before the enemy could find it.

Night vision technology was still new, and the scopes in use at the time worked by gathering available light from the night sky. They worked fairly well, certainly well enough to make it important to keep the instrument out of the hands of the enemy.

We flew out to the west again, while I sat in the open doorway in order to see all I could of the land—any rivers, breaks in the endless knap of trees, or any promontories—by which to orient an unassisted escape in case we were compromised on the ground. I had learned to see more, to better gauge the probable contour of the ground, but it was always mostly conjecture, guessing down through a continental featurelessness that cannot be imagined by anyone who has never seen it. This time the shoreless botanical ocean that lapped beneath us mocked my effort.

Having learned little by the time we over-flew the brown scar in the jungle that marked our objective, I had then to contend again with those chilling squads of fear that invariably welled within me as the chopper began its descent. Since we did not know what, if any, investigation of the site had been (or was being) conducted by the enemy, and due to the paucity of insertion points in the area where the battle had taken place, we could not be landed at the site itself, or even conveniently close to it.

This time we had to rappel hurriedly down through the trees while the choppers hovered, which as far as I could see, meant that we were clearly showing our insertion point to any observer. Our only clear option for eventual extraction would be the objective itself—a large scar in the landscape I had seen from the air. It looked to be about four or five miles away, which further raised the stakes of its timely discovery. If we all made it down without mishap, it would be a long slog at the pace we had to move, perhaps as much as a week.

Once settled on the ground we crawled slowly, cautiously, for three and a half days southwestward, creeping stealthily toward, what? I didn't know enough. We were making for a place that had been ravaged by an air strike. We were supposed to scour a large area of wilderness burned by napalm and otherwise in unknown condition for an object about 4" by maybe 18", which was possibly mounted on a rifle. The odds against our finding it amid the destruction lay beyond reasoned calculation, and if the bad guys knew about our objective they were very likely looking too, assuming they had not already captured it. The whole operation seemed hopeless, and although my feelings about pointless risk were by now familiar, they did nothing to lessen a sense of the dangers assembled in places of known interest to the enemy.

There was another feeling too, an oppressive, generalized perception of endlessness, a distortion of reasonable expectations, constantly reborn from integrated layers of threat that seemed to drag on in a ceaseless drudgery of re-emergence without resolution. Nor could I escape the feeling of entrapment between the colliding agendas of disparate bureaucracies and their inexplicable correlated vagaries, wherein the high art of stealth for days on end in a stifling jungle, and its costs in time and emotion, simply raised the price of any interim conclusions I could draw from the available evidence, while no resolution ever seemed to come, and the reward for survival was just to be sent out again.

The sense of expectancy was a conditioned impulse that gradually, little by little, bogged you down. There was never any feeling that you were safe and none that some dependable outcome would result. Quite the contrary. The reward for sharpening your jungle skills, for training your senses and forcing an inner resolve kept receding, and slowly the notion that the iniquity was provisional gave way to the feeling that it may be endless. Nothing could be conclusive for there was no grip, no evidence, by which a leavening realization could be seized. The feeling, once acknowledged, spread like a gray leprosy, and it left me crawling on the jungle floor with the last remnants of my initial belief that I might survive unraveling in a tattered weft of abandoned hope.

A warm rain soaked us briefly on the fourth day, adding to the misery of our condition and reopening old chafing wounds under the pack straps across my shoulders. We were hot, dirty, thirsty, and now, between the dripping vegetation and mucid black compost of the jungle floor through which we had to move mostly on our hands and knees and to belly crawl, our fatigues were saturated with rain water, ammoniac sweat, and wet earth. I strained to listen to any sound of movement while tiny insects whined in my ears and plagued my eyes.

The tangled undergrowth made for extremely slow going. We were forced for much of our progress onto the ground itself, creeping like animals among the stems and roots to keep below the congestion of vines. I did my best to scrape the mud from the closure snaps on my ammunition pouches and other equipment, washing my fingers when I could in the run-off from the leaves.

Just before evening came down, the jungle began to reveal signs of having been recently disturbed. It was strange to see such evidence after the deep sense of isolation and abandonment that our days in the wild had imposed. There was a freshly broken stem here and there, torn leaves, trampled ground cover, and occasional projectile injury to the trees. It was impossible to tell who or what had caused the damage. It could mean we were approaching the objective, or it could be signs of some other engagement entirely. We might have come across the path of enemy movement made by a body of men who could still be close by.

We went on increased alert, the whole team just melting soundlessly into the shadows, where we lay listening and watching for any movement. As we waited the shadows deepened. The light that filtered feebly through the canopy quickly withdrew to make room for a thick, viscous darkness.

We stayed where we were, enclosed by large trees, and formed ourselves for the RON on wet ground. I wasn't looking forward to whatever we were likely to encounter, if indeed what we had seen so far were indications that we were nearing the objective. I knew we would be subject to the risks that attended our last operation to open ground, with little likelihood of recovering a lone Starlight scope in whatever remained of a deep jungle air strike that had happened some five days before. I worried about how much time we would have to spend in such a place of likely interest to the enemy in order to do a sufficiently thorough search for me to answer the questions I'd be asked in the after-action report.

I ate a ball of gritty rice and tried to plan through all the unknowns, but there just wasn't enough information. I settled into the mud for the night, sending the filaments of my attention outward.

Around us the leaves dribbled from the recent rain, the droplets falling in loud splats and then trailing off in blubbering runnels. It was familiar on one entirely physical level, but even as my understanding of the jungle grew, I knew that I would never come to truly know it. Even after days of fearful observation and the studied movements that it demanded, I knew I was really only seeing its surface. It always withheld the essential nature of its moods, day or night, light and shadow. It's difficult to put into words that hugely metaphysical quality that it whispers to you in a voice too vast and deep for human hearing the full history you think it tells.

The fresh moisture had released a complex of smells that rose as darkness fell. The strong odor of rot in the damp earth intensified, but there soon seemed to be the breath of other things carried on the muggy air. I sensed burnt vegetation and turned earth, a hint of cordite, and then-the unmistakable sickly eminence of death. In the gathering gloom, I had seen no sign of a clearing ahead, but I could hear the Nungs sniffing and realized that we had all picked up on the evidence and knew we were near the site of something bad.

The complex salad of rancid odors grew as we worked our careful approach the next morning. Grayish light through the trees ahead soon gave way to open sky and a great sagging canopy of coming rain, plump and low. As we emerged, beneath the clouds was revealed a landscape of the Last Judgment. It required a long minute to grasp the scene and the implications of what it contained. The earth was churned, torn, scorched, layered over with still smoke, and strewn with the blackened remains of dead humans. Parts of bodies protruded from the furrowed ground amid the skeletons of shattered trees, some shivered off at the base of the trunk, many others with a single grotesque and hopeless branch left. Nothing moved. The place still radiated heat and had been swept clean of living things by a tempest of orchestral death. There were no birds. Even the air was stilled.

Dull points of light glinted weakly throughout from a rain of empty aviation cannon brasses and the torn metal of burst napalm containers. Numerous oblong craters of different sizes reflected the sky in standing brown water through a thin pall of gray smoke that fed upon scattered wisps drifting forth uncertainly from different places, some from the bodies, a few of which still cooked. The putrid, all-pervasive smell of rotting meat hung over everything.

Hostage of Paradox by John Rixey Moore

We waited a long time, taking in the devastation and watching for any movement. Then, keeping under cover, we skirted with great care about half the clearing, surveying the destruction from different vantage points and gradually coming to believe that we were, at least for now, alone there.

Such places were taboo to both sides and with good reason. In addition to the horrible collection of violent deaths, swarms of disease-bearing flies that arrived to feed together on both the living and the dead were a strong deterrent. In addition, air strikes on collected infantry produced an omnipresent blanket of putrefaction that saturated every breath. I began to think that these things would probably serve to make it a fairly protected RON site, at least discouraging of enemy incursion. I tied my tourniquet around my nose and mouth, bandit-style, the earthy smell of the fabric delivering some relief from the rotten air.

Yet the scene held a morbid fascination. There were long minutes when I couldn't tear my eyes away from it. It gripped my attention, insisting that I look. It wanted me to take it all in, make it a part of my living consciousness and of whatever might remain of my own uncertain life. Even in the thrall of its present evidence I found it hard to imagine the full horror of being on the receiving end of a napalm attack. I thought how the sacrifice of another people for one's own strategic aims was a fearful thing indeed when one was down here among those being sacrificed. I felt an intense surrogate kind of fear of what I was seeing, as though just looking might somehow connect me with this kind of violence. It was notably reminiscent of old sepia photographs of the terrible devastation on the Somme and in Ypres at Passchendaele in WWI, but here, it was the religious intensity of the smells that animated such a garbled and poignant fascination.

Nearby, a tangled row of roasted corpses, busy with flies, lay thrown together, their swollen trunks like burned sausages, and among them was a severed head that faced us with its strange half-lidded look of grotesque *ennui* into which the features had dried. It seemed to whisper that the facile recourse to violence that our technology has introduced in the 20th century experience had given us a new Dark Age.

The ground had been so churned by the air strike that it was difficult to tell where the American ground force had been positioned. We had to locate their old line if we were to have any chance of finding the scope. Judging by the angle at which most of the craters had been made, it appeared that the aircraft had come in from the north, the same direction as we had. This meant that the Americans had probably not been at the southern end or our planes would have been firing toward them. I had to guess that any signs of the U.S. position would have to be some distance back from either the northern end of the clearing or from the east or west sides, assuming the aircraft had been called in roughly parallel to the friendly front—a pure guess. Everything was so torn up that it was very hard to tell anything certain from our limited perspective. If I was guessing right, though, the bodies we encountered near the northern end seemed out of place. This indicated the limitations of my guesswork and that we had most of the perimeter to explore, possibly leaving only the southern edge, and that would take much more time than I wanted to linger in this dreadful place. I didn't like the prospect. The going promised to be difficult work.

The others by now had wrapped their faces in tourniquets, and thus struggling through the sickening air, we continued making our way around the site, adding to our defensive scan a search of the ground for any abandoned U.S. equipment, dropped gear, rifle brass, signs of the firefight and withdrawal. We found nothing, not even burned rifle brass. I guessed that either we had worked our way down the wrong side, or the Americans had been farther away than I assumed, or perhaps they had withdrawn before the air strike, and evidence of their position had been obliterated in the wreckage of the site.

By late afternoon we had crept, stumbled and crawled with great difficulty all the way around to the southern end of the burn, which I had speculated initially to have been the most likely position of the enemy. The few artifacts we collected had indicated no pattern. Just at the edge of the trees, we came upon an impact crater that had thrown up a pile of ejected earth near the base of a half-burned tree. There, in a hollow at the top of the little hill it made, sat a dead Vietnamese machine gunner behind the ruins of his weapon. The top of his head had been blown off and the brain-pan was full of rainwater. We stopped to rest here as the trees were particularly dense, and we were all exhausted. I relieved myself of the radio and propped it at the base of a tree. Because this location was slightly higher than the rest of the site, Nhi and I risked exposure by crawling up the backside of the blast mound to scan the open area with binoculars.

Except for the air bending in heat vapor, nothing moved anywhere but the insects that darted against the dark wall of the jungle. As we continued to wait and to watch the stagnant surroundings, we began to amuse ourselves by idly trying to flick pebbles into the corpse's head. Every now and then one of us would be rewarded by a satisfying little *plerk* noise from the target pool.

After a time, as we continued trying for greater accuracy, it dawned on me what I was doing. How, I wondered, had I come to this? When did the line begin to blur between the person I had been and the one who was here now whiling a few distracted minutes in this macabre little game? What were the steps by which I had come into this shadow world where the quick and the dead exist in such intimate embrace, where the dead might offer themselves for a moment of quiet amusement? Had I really closed off my capacity for horror to the extent that I could so parcel my attention for greater threats; and then: what part of my mind was able to stand apart from this moment to pose the question? Perhaps I had simply wanted to do something harmlessly entertaining, some brief activity I could actually control, and thus enjoy a fleeting illusion of power over all that was frightening, unseen and dangerous.

I had been pushed progressively nearer some metaphysical brink than I ever expected to go, had crossed an un-sensed boundary where the seed of personality had become lost in the cumulative nature of lethal congruences and incremental austerities. Much later, I would come to realize that, however childish I might remain, actual youth had been pressed out of me in those dark, interminable hours and over the months of baneful operations in that malignant and endless wilderness.

These thoughts were suddenly arrested by a sound, a faint noise more felt than heard, little more than a scurry in the mind. I stopped and strained to hear. Nothing. Nhi went rigid too. After a few cavernous moments of whispery insect sounds, it returned. This time, it burbled hesitantly on the stagnant air as nothing more than a tiny, plaintive bleat, almost like something newborn far off, but too veiled by the dense vegetation to judge the distance.

With that, we both jumped, instant voltage. It could have been some kind of animal voice; I couldn't be sure. In any case it filtered through the normal jungle sounds like a scratch on the silence. The team behind us tensed, and two of them looked off to the left. It sounded as though it might have come from that direction, and for the moment their stares seemed to endorse the instinct. My temples pounded in the charged uncertainty as we waited, urging our senses through the stillness. I forced a yawn to clear my ears. It could have been the muted croak of some small burrower or a tree lizard. Sometimes even burned or rotting vegetation would expel a release of gas with soft, eerie sighs that could haunt the sanctums of the forest in the night and leave a man huddled in his poncho liner on the ground trembling in a private hell of fear and longing.

Then I heard it again. A thin, wavering cry rose and fell, barely audible, a twisted thread plucked from the sleeve of silence, little more than a tentative assertion in the negative of the day. It died once more, leaving no echo, only a kind of soundless mimicry of its quaver, the empty shadow of a noise. I still couldn't tell what we had heard. Apart from its strangeness, I wasn't sure in the silence that followed if we had heard anything other than perhaps a bird. Parrots could sound unnervingly like the cry of a child. Except that the Chinese, by the tenor of their stares, had obviously been alerted to something they couldn't identify either, and they didn't like it. They were strung taut.

Alarm raced through us all in a bolt of morphic resonance, and Nhi and I slipped back down the muddy berm into the shadows. I thumbed the safety off and signaled for the team to spread out, assigning one to watch out behind us in the opposite direction. We began to creep through the palpable stillness in the direction of the strange mewl, keeping low to the jungle floor and with all receptors on full alert. After covering 30 meters or so of torturous movement through the tangle of downed trees and twisted undergrowth, another cry tugged again at the fearful quiet. It was close. We stopped. Listened. Then we saw it. About 15 feet away lay a body on the ground in burned clothing amid a swarm of flies. It twitched, and we drew down on it as we approached.

He was in the tattered remains of American fatigues, the scorched fabric greasy and dark with old blood. He had been shot and burned, his skin horribly discolored, red veined and purpled, and there were places where it had peeled from his limbs in dried sleavings. Had I known him I would not have recognized the damaged face. His eyes were sunken, the lids drooped at different levels, and what little awareness remained in them seemed to have receded far beyond the threshold of sanity. With him on the ground, blackened and muddy, was the rifle with the Starlight scope.

Here was what we had come for with such tremendous odds against finding anything. This poor guy had probably been sent forward at night with the scope, and his buddies, perhaps having heard the shot that wounded him, and unwilling or unable to send out a patrol to find him the next morning, had withdrawn in the desperate confusion of the air strike without him. Wounded, perhaps before the pull-out, and without medical attention or food for all this time, he must have realized at some point after the terror of the napalm drop that he had been abandoned, yet had somehow managed to drag himself to this lost place. I hoped for his sake he was not aware, but our presence over him with our weapons made the last of his misery, for his eyes flicked at us, he gazed vacantly for a moment, then a dark leer of madness set his face, his arm made a strange embryonic gesture, and his head dropped back onto the ground. His mouth stirred and released a sound, a burble of noise for which there is no word, just a soaked orphan of the alphabet. He tried to roll over and was dead. I could tell by the way the body seemed to subside, as though something had been let out of it, that he was gone. Perhaps on some level he had been waiting for the moment when his friends would return.

We quickly gathered up the scope and pulled the body to a sitting position so that I could get my shoulder under it. The slumped weight was greater than I expected and the cold skin greasy. I staggered up with it and we moved back through the heavy pestiferous air to our position just inside the tree line. The corpse was a gruesome burden, creepy and hard to balance, until breathless and near collapse, I got back to where I could set it down beneath the half-burned tree by the dirt mound. Some of his skin had stuck to my equipment. I sucked at the muggy, death-laden air, and with my vision swimming and the ventricles pulsing in my chest, realized that I was probably suffering a loss of strength from the initial stages of malnutrition. I had to sit down and put my head between my knees to arrest the dizziness.

I can still feel him there across my shoulders. Once you've carried a dead person, I guess he'll always be there, riding with you. It's true, almost unbearably so, that close exposure to the dead sensitizes you to the force of their presence. That day, I think we all felt the weirdness of finding him and realizing the strange circumstances of his being in the place he had crawled to in his terrible pain and unthinkable despair. Now at least he was past hope, past care. Had he lived, he would probably have been doomed to wait out his existence in some VA hospital, a deranged husk, with burned skin tightening, encasing his body in a slow prison of integument.

I took his dog tags and a few incidentals from his pockets. I checked the scope. It was damaged beyond use, but at least we were able to recover it. I wondered what would happen to the poor guy's company commander when it was learned that we found his man alive.

I turned on the radio and sent the codes for extraction, giving as our location the site of the objective. By then, it was too late in the day to come for us, so I also sent that we would RON on site. Lastly I transmitted the code for one dead, hoping the implication this carried for the team itself would produce an emergency launch for our extraction first thing in the morning.

We were all at the end of our strength. I was shivering with fatigue and nervous strain when we set up for the night and, as usual, suffering the debilities that are the inevitable price of sleep deprivation. I was not at all sure how I would hold up through another day in the grim authority of this place where quantum death, the muddy stench of rot, and the insidious pervasion of finality commanded the senses.

Awaiting extraction from the field was always strenuous. Because of the need to turn the squelch control on the radio so far down, I was never sure my messages were getting through. Worse, this time we were deep in wet vegetation, especially bad for signal strength, although any jungle will cut the range of transmission. I ran the antenna out into the open edge of the burn, hoping to send in relatively unobstructed air, but there would be no sign of success until we might hear the faint beat of the big Sikorskys thumping slowly nearer in the distance.

Low clouds brought an early end to daylight, and sudden rain swept in through the trees to usher out the last of it. We covered the pitiful corpse and its weight of sadness with a rubber poncho, which rattled in the fall of rain most of the night, lending the quiet thing beneath it a discomforting voice. It demanded of us the attention it had been denied. None of us slept.

4

Eyes Only
by R. S. Carlson

We're in the A-75th Support mess hall, scraping
pork and beans off paper plates when Simmons
waves his plastic fork in the air, stops to
belch, then starts to bug Oakley...

Ya know, you code jockeys ain't the only ones in
the unit to handle some hot stuff. I got a really
hot item in this morning in secure comms for . . .
Simmons! Can it!

(That's from Oakley who can't let anybody
forget that it could be five years in
Leavenworth and a ten thousand smacker
fine for breaching security.)

Yah, Oakley. So here's a pen and a napkin.
Transcribe this yourself for the court martial,
O.K. Big Guy? Make sure you get it down
verbatim, and note that I've stolen that pen, too!

So, while you guys are breaking out all the lies
the NVA lieutenants in the field are feeding their
rear-area major about how they're wiping the ARVN
off Ba Ho, I'm bringing in big news from HQ.
Like I said, it comes in secure commo from the

Commanding General, I Corps to Brigade HQ,
Classified Secret: SPARK—Eyes Only. It's the
real dope on the stand-down of U.S. units along the DMZ.

By now all the guys are tilted to Simmons except
Oakley who has a few words scribbled on the
napkin but is waiting to see whether Simmons is
just blowing smoke to string him along.

Ready guys? C'mon, Oakley. Get this quote.
"URGENT YOU SEND CRYSTAL, CHINA AND GOLD
TABLE SERVICE FROM YOUR OFFICERS' MESS TO
OFFICERS' MESS THIS HQ SOONEST."

Hey, Oakley. Won't that help the VC? How're you
gonna make hard-stripe sergeant if you don't write
down every last word of my big breach for CID? Here,
let me put your paper plate in the trash for you.

Great essay —

Titles
by Earl Smallwood, Jr.

Retired. Retired is my title now. Over the years, everyone has many, many titles. For over 40 years I have had the title of father and husband. Even though there was a brief break in the husband title. My first wife finally decided she had had enough of my outrageous behavior and decided it was time for me to have the title of divorced. Fortunately, a few years later I met a wonderful woman who found my outrageous behavior cute and reinstated my title of husband.

As I go back over my life, titles of manager, buyer, sales associate, teacher, administrator, friend, brother all come to my mind. Some titles are not near as flattering as others. Titles like selfish, irresponsible and racist are not descriptions that a person is proud of but they are titles nonetheless. Some titles are earned, some titles are inherited and some titles just happen. One title that I acquired many years ago was Army recruit. This is one of those titles that I actually "volunteered" for. I didn't know it at the time but the title of Army recruit drastically change forever the titles I would have for the rest of my life.

I have very vivid memories of how this new title was attained. It was December 1967, and I was sitting in my now deceased older sister's house. I had just been on a job interview for the title of door-to-door encyclopedia salesman. These were the only interviews a male with a 1-A military classification could find. I had tried the college student title but the partying proved just too overwhelming for me. So, here I am in my sister's house and she says, "Why don't you just join the Army"? I looked at her with this horrified expression and said, "Don't you know there is a war going on and I could die"? My sister's response was the most classic line ever, "Well, just don't die. Do whatever it takes to live through it." Those words and the conversation we had hit me like a Mickey Mantle line drive. The military was my only option and a reality that I had created for myself. I left my sister's house with a new attitude and a new course of action. My next stop would be the recruiting office in my local area.

The weather, like in most stories, was typical winter weather—cold, windy and just downright miserable—as I brought my beautiful '62 Chevy Coupe to a stop in the parking lot of the local Army recruiting office. My sense of self-preservation and common sense had kicked in now and I knew that this was a really bad idea. Just before entering the building, I gave myself an "options" check. What can I do? Where can I go, is there anything else I can do?

The answer unfortunately to all was "No." The recruiter was a nice enough fellow with lots of blink on his chest and stripes on his sleeve. After the introductions, the recruiter began to paint this wonderful picture of life in the Army and the opportunities the Army provided. I interrupted the gentleman in mid-sentence and said, "What titles in the Army are the safest in Vietnam? I do not intend to make a career of the military, I just want to survive my tour in Vietnam." My sister's words were planted firmly in the front of my brain and I intended to comply with those words. The response from the recruiter almost made me laugh. "The safest jobs in Vietnam are cook and clerk-typist," replied the recruiter with a little smirk of his face. Obviously, he was looking for a gun-toting, knife-in-the-teeth killer, but the guy in front of him was far from that. My mind was already racing. Cook, clerk-typist, really? No 20-year-old stud wants to be kitchen help or a girly, girly typist. I thought, Well guys at the front have to eat just like guys in the rear so cook is out. I had taken typing in high school so I could hang with the chicks and I felt I could type my way through the war better that shooting my way through the war. "Clerk typist it is," I said to the recruiter and all conversation ended. Out came the paperwork, I signed on the dotted line and my new title was Army recruit.

It is now January 1968, and I'm on a bus to Ft. Benning, Georgia. As we arrive at our departure area, I immediately realize I had several new titles. Dumbass, stupid and worthless were the first three titles the drill instructor gave us as we exited the bus for our first day in the Army. WOW, I could tell immediately that this was going to be an interesting adventure. For eight weeks, the drill instructors belittled, cussed and abused us from early morning until late, late at night. As we went through the various training routines, my sister's words were always close by. When we took the battery of tests to determine abilities, skills and aptitude, I was always mindful of the traps laid within the questions. Do you like to camp? Are you sure-footed? Do you like to hunt? A "yes" response to these were certain to put a gun in my hand. On the gun range, I scored 2 above the minimum required to complete the course even though I had been around guns all my life. Well, graduation finally arrived and I was off to my next adventure. I had in fact earned the right to go to clerk-typist school. The unfortunate part was, it was at Ft. Leonard Wood, Missouri.

My clerk-typist school experience was pretty uneventful. We spent our days learning to type, arrange sentences and how to correctly punctuate. All this came easy to me because of my 2 years of typing in high school. I survived all the traps and pitfalls of this school but many did not. If you failed any of the many, many tests and rules that came with this school, you were immediately shipped off to combat school. There were always openings in combat school. Fortunately, no opening for me. We gleefully graduated from clerk-typist school and awaited our next assignment. As luck would have it, my orders came for Vietnam. Go figure. I've been in the Army less than six months and I'm headed for Hell.

Now it is time to take my new title, clerk-typist, pack my bag and head to Vietnam. The plane ride overseas was a cool 20 hours and gives a person lots of opportunity for reflection and speculation. I kept telling myself that everything will be OK. I was in the top three graduates from my class and thinking surely they wouldn't send me out in the field. We will just have to wait and see. As luck would have it, the air base where we landed was being shelled as we landed. So the NCO in charge of us tells us to get off the plane and run like hell to the buses parked about 150 yards away. Have you ever run 150 yards with a full duffel bag hung from you shoulder? My first thought was, I'm not even going to make it off the plane! We all survived and made it to the busses. We arrived at the processing center and for several days waited around for our new assignment. While we were waiting, most of us filled the hours by filling sandbags, hundreds of sandbags. I was filling sandbags when a fellow soldier came up to me with a message that I should go clean up and put on my best green fatigues because I had an interview at USARV headquarters. USARV headquarters was where the command and control function of the Army was handled. My interview went well and I now had a new title, "typist for the Campaign Planning Group." Sounds cool, huh?

When I arrived at my new job, I was amazed to find out that I was the only enlisted man in the organization. The boss was a full bird colonel with four lieutenant colonels and four majors working for him. I had never seen so much brass in my life. Each and every one of these officers treated me as an equal even though clearly they were way over my head. We were a team whose job it was to create a plan for the orderly withdrawal of US forces from Vietnam. Obviously, my job was not to create but to type the procedure. We toiled day and night on this project. One interesting side note to this was that a top secret security clearance was required to do this job. The FBI spent two weeks in my hometown checking every part of my background and I still got the clearance. It took us over 8 months to come up with the plan. During that time, we had to give briefings to the Secretary of the Army, the Commanding General of the Army (General Abrams) and many, many other dignitaries. My job was to handle the slide show that accompanied the presentation. It was amazing stuff. After many rewrites, the plan was finally finished and submitted to the top military commanders and politicians who were running the war. To my amazement, this plan, the one that I had typed was presented to the President of the United States, Richard Nixon. During Nixon's televised address to the US population about the situation in Vietnam, he read verbatim from the proposal that I had spent my entire tour in Vietnam typing. I took great pride in that fact, knowing that I was a small part of history. It was only a matter of weeks until my tour in Vietnam was over and I had another title, Vietnam Veteran. I had made it through and my sister's words were still in my head. "Don't die."

6

A Recurrent Case of Plasmatic Parasitosis Flashback 1968
by Jeffrey Alan Rochlin

The cadence caller's ghost inside my head chants,
mud & blood & guts & gore
the reapers creep'in up my back door
stains of brains on head wound holes
in class VI stores* I drown my souls

Every day I cradle death
on battlegrounds
where seared flesh dredged in DNA
crackles in the sun
till meat rots off the bone

clear the airway
stop the bleeding
decipher triage tutorials
on endless disassembly lines
dead men don't bleed
I try to coddle life

first blood trickles
then it seeps
then runs
then spurts
then gushes

Returning Soldiers Speak

my hands
useless levees against the flood
I swirl down
into body fluid burial grounds

march in a *Cadence Callers Dirge*
to the creeks of battle wearied bones
where skinned facades of soldiers sleep
in sod and soil memorials

If I die before they wake
let the devil eat my birthday cake
I pray the earth my soul to take

Rochlin, Jeffrey Alan
Medic Specialist 4th Class
US56718963 Row 19 Plot 32
Veterans Memorial Cemetery
Westwood, Calif.
*military base liqueur stores

7

June 7, 1968
by James F. Miller

I was a young, 22-year-old old officer in the Navy. I was the X.O. of a five-man team Special Forces, SEAL Team.

We were fifteen clicks out of Da Nang on a mop-up, after the VC had gone through and executed an entire village. As we were walking in the village I could see men, women, and even children just lying there dead in their tracks. Some shot in the head, some in the back. I was in shock to see a dead mother still holding on to her dead child. It was like a dream state and everything was in slow motion. The VC had killed over sixty-three people.

We gathered in the middle of the village to discuss our next plan of attack. We decided to gather the dead in one central location. As I looked around for a high point to keep watch, my C.O. supervised the three men with the gruesome duty of gathering the bodies.

I found a tree suitable for recon.

It seemed like I had been up that tree for hours but in fact it had only been about forty minutes. All of a sudden something caught my attention from the north. It was a young girl about 10 or 11 years of age. She looked like she was a village survivor, or was she somebody new? I was not able to tell the difference from three hundred yards out. I signaled my C.O. and he passed the word around the men to take up locations. They did, blending into the dense jungle. I took a better position on the tree, and when I signaled my C.O. that she was about thirty-five yards away, he gave me the signal to bring her down.

That was the signal I did not want. Now I was wishing I were moving the d.b.'s (dead bodies) and one of the other men would take this shot. I had not killed anyone but I knew I would have to one day. I had been no more than three weeks in-country. By this time the girl was about 25-yards away. She had a cold look on her face. I was in a cold sweat, my hair on the back of my neck started to stand up. I reached for my .45 and locked my eyes on her. She locked her eyes with mine and just kept walking towards me.

Her hands were behind her back.

I squeezed the trigger and shot her in the forehead. Her eyes rolled back and turned white before her body started to fall. Her head and her body exploded from behind her.

It turned out she had a hand grenade behind her back. She was willing to use it on us while sacrificing herself in the process.

It was June 7, 1968, at approximately 14:23. I was young, twenty-two. X.O. of a 5-man team. It was my third week in-country and my first sight of death.

That day was the day I grew up and innocence was left behind in that village. Sixty-five people died there that day and I killed a young girl and she killed my soul at the same time. I have never been the same since. There were more after that, but that young girl—that is one face I have seen every day for over forty years.

I wake up every night in a cold sweat.

She did not affect the other soldiers as much as she did me because they didn't look in her eyes like I did. They didn't see her eyes turn white with death like I did.

It was so hard to write this down. But I decided to write to let the civilians know that when a veteran—a warrior—returns from combat, that soldier needs a very strong support group not only from the Veterans Administration but also from their families and friends.

Try to understand this for your child, brother, sister, or a family member, or even a friend. They need for you to understand.

I need for you to understand.

8

Late Summer of '68
by James F. Miller

I had been in-country for about 2 1/2 months. I had earned the respect of my men. I had proven myself to them in several encounters with the VC. This particular day stands out only because of the irony of what happened.

We were at the Cambodia/Vietnam border when we were told by Intel that there was a village nearby held by VC. We approached the village with caution. We entered the village from the south. We had just begun the out-swipe. Three men went inside as we remained outside keeping guard. As the men came out we started getting fired upon from the north. We scrambled for cover. I dove behind a tree. There were four hooches that had VC in them. I took aim at the hooch to the left of the village. I started to fire my AK. We used AK's due to the fact it was hard to get ammo for our M-16s. My fire was concentrated on the first hooch and I quickly emptied six clips one right after another.

The firefight seemed to me like it lasted for an eternity but in reality it lasted no longer than five minutes.

After the firing stopped, we began the dangerous task of making sure that all VC were dead. We separated into 2-man teams. Two men stood watch by the trees because it was the best position to view all four hooches in case some VC had survived the firefight. My partner and I went to the first hooch, the other pair started at the third hooch.

As my partner and I approached with caution, I had trouble swallowing and my heartbeat was loud and I was not able to hear anything else. I looked at my partner and signaled him that I would go in and for him to approach the window from the outside.

As I entered the hooch the first thing I saw was a man lying with a boy about age four or five. The man's head was half gone and the boy's body was riddled with my bullets. The man was still holding on to his weapon with his son lying at his feet. As I checked around I heard a scream of a woman under a table. I moved the table ready to fire without any hesitation, and to my surprise I saw a woman ready to give birth at any minute. She was going into labor right there, right next to her dead son and dead husband. She pointed to her crotch between contractions. She put her legs up. I had grown up on a ranch and had seen new life being birthed but from farm animals. This was the first time I would see a woman give birth.

I walked around her, keeping my AK pointed at her head. As I came to her feet I noticed the baby was crowning. I quickly called out to my partner to go get Doc. That was our medic; we called him "Doc" because he was the closest thing we had to a doctor in the field. I proceeded to lay down my weapon and I made hand gestures to her to follow my breathing pattern, and then I got in front of her on my knees. With nothing but my bare hands, I was holding the baby's head and was more nervous than I had ever been before. I hadn't done this before. I was scared to death that I would hurt the baby, crush it, break it or screw it up. I kept the baby supported by the head but the woman was giving up. I kept telling her to push as I grabbed the baby by the shoulders and pulled her out. I was holding a newborn baby girl in my arms. The mother was so happy to see the baby she had just given birth to. She extended her arms out signaling me to hand her over. As I did she proceeded to look the baby over. The mother looked at both her feet and hands.

I am no doctor but I knew the baby's lungs were fine. The young newborn, born into this hellhole, was screaming from the top of her lungs just right after she passed through the birth canal.

I looked at the mother as she held her baby in her arms.

The young mother looked at me and with a heavy broken accent said, "Thank you," and smiled.

Then the young mother pointed to her dead son's neck and signaled me that she wanted the necklace around the boy's neck.

I took it off and rinsed the blood off with water and handed it to her. She smiled and placed the cross around the baby's neck.

At that point Doc entered and looked at the baby then at me and as he proceeded to attend to the mother he said, "Good job, LT."

Doc quickly tied the umbilical cord and cut it and nothing went wrong with the delivery. Doc managed to speak with her in Vietnamese and found out that her sister and mother lived in a village not far from where we were. We made a litter of bamboo and rope so we could transport her and the baby.

On the way back to our camp I was thinking that this young woman had lost her husband and son not knowing that I had killed them but was so grateful for the new life I had just helped her bring into this miserable war! The feelings that came to me at that moment were hope! Hope that this baby girl makes it through this war and that she will never experience or remember any of what her dead brother saw!

9

My First Christmas in Vietnam
by James F. Miller

I had just turned twenty-three years old on December 12, 1968. While on a search-and-destroy mission, my five-man SEAL team I was in charge of, was dispatched to travel to a location about five miles from where we were and locate and bring back two downed F-4 pilots. The location was in Cambodia and even though we were never officially in Cambodia, I spent most of my time there.

We spread out in a crossing pattern /X/X/X/X/X/ searching for any sign of them. I was on point to the left of the team when I spotted a parachute in a rice paddy. I figured a pilot was attached to the chute.

Just as I entered a clump of bamboo in the water I heard a noise to my right. Six VC had burst through the foliage. All I could think to do was cut a bamboo reed and lay down in the paddy, praying I would be able to breathe. The reed I grabbed was four to five feet tall and there was no time to check for knots. Thank goodness the bamboo was clear inside so I could breathe through it while under the water.

I couldn't hear but I could see them make camp, eat, and post sentries while the others slept. I didn't move, didn't flinch. I was scared to death. I was scared to death for three tours of duty. I was trained to accept fear as your best asset. Fear keeps you sharp, heightens your senses.

All I was concerned with was being able to breathe through the reed. I could deal with the VC if they found me. I had my AK-47 aimed at the surface. They would have been real surprised by a shooting fish!

After almost nineteen hours under water the six decided to break camp and vanished just as suddenly as they had appeared. I was covered in leeches and let me to tell you, leeches suck even when they suck on something they shouldn't.

I double-timed the five miles up a steady incline to the landing zone. It seemed like I got there in seven minutes. I knew I was fast but I didn't think I was *that* fast.

The rest of my team had located our flyboys and had waited at the pre-arranged landing zone for me to show up.

I arrived approximately one half hour prior to sending up the balloon for the snatch and grab. Both pilots had to be snatched with the same balloon, as there was no time to deploy a second one. We had to tie them together with a rope so they wouldn't collide in mid-air when the plane came for the grab.

After the snatch we vanished into the jungle as if we were never there.

This was my first Christmas away from my family and one I will never forget.

10

...Take One Down, Pass It Around...
by R. S. Carlson

Hayes was soused and smoked past talking.
I took my Orange Crush from the club shack
to my hootch and dropped on my cot. It did my back
no better than a hammock. Next hootch was rocking
with a girl till neighboring brass yelled warning:
"MPs are on patrol!" With quiet,
I relaxed, expecting sleep. Right.
Some new guy brought the hooker in, turning
on his light, fumbling with his fly
and belt, drunk, and wanting this to be
her sweetest. Only paid for five, and sore
from dozens extra, she begged for no more,
him chanting "What's wrong?" while she
moaned, "Too many G.I. . . . Too many G.I. . . ."

11

Enemy
by Michael Sadler

I was a 20-year old U.S. Navy triage corpsman at the military support hospital on the outskirts of the second largest city in South Vietnam, Da Nang, just south of the Demilitarized Zone. My job during the entire year of 1969 was to sort, prioritize, and provide emergency medical treatment—mostly to U.S. Marines who came in by helicopter off the field. Our triage unit was not exactly Cedars Sinai Medical Center—rather a corrugated steel Quonset hut with gurneys on both sides and medical supplies. There were a dozen corpsman at a time in 24-hour on/24-hour off rotation, plus a single triage doctor. No nurses were assigned to triage.

We treated anyone who needed treatment, including civilians. And also the occasional prisoner of war—or POW.

In Vietnam, the enemy came basically in two forms: the first were the Viet Cong. VC. Victor Charley. The Cong. These were the local insurgents who worked their rice paddies by day and their AK-47's and booby-traps by night. The second were North Vietnamese Army regulars, or NVA—"professional" soldiers recruited and trained in the north, and then sent south to fight.

In the fall of 1969, during one particularly heavy afternoon influx of Marine casualties, I was coming down from x-ray and spotted two military interrogators standing over a wounded POW, an NVA regular lying on a stretcher, his left knee heavily bandaged. He was in a separate area outside the triage Quonset hut, cordoned off by saw-horses and yellow tape.

I'd seen only a handful of NVA regulars at our facility, as they were usually transported directly to a local Vietnamese hospital. For reasons unknown to me, then and now, this POW was brought to our facility for treatment. But a little Intel for the interrogators prior to surgery seemed an urgent matter. I passed by them several times and could hear only bits of the conversation as one of the interrogators spoke in flawless Vietnamese. But it showed up to me as the classic Good-Cop/Bad-Cop scenario working its magic over there. The POW seemed cooperative, to a point, agreeing with certain things, denying or negating others.

At one point, the lead interrogator grabbed the POW by his collar and shook him while yelling a few inches from his face, then slapped him. Not hard, but enough to get his attention. The POW *was* paying attention—and I could see by his face, and hear by his stressed out voice, that he was clearly terrified.

Injured Marines had first priority when it came to treatment, so the POW had to wait at least an hour before time and resources to treat him became available.

After things quieted down in triage, with all the surgical bays filled with wounded Marines, plus a few others awaiting surgery in pre-op, I walked over to the interrogators and asked them if they were finished with their questioning. They said yes, and pointed out his injury—a single rifle bullet had blasted out his kneecap. The POW was in a lot of pain, and I asked if he'd been given anything for it. No, not yet, the lead guy said, because they wanted him coherent for interrogation. Fair enough. They even offered that he'd been pretty cooperative.

That POW wasn't going anywhere on his own, so they turned him over to me and went to the mess hall for a good meal. And from that moment until I released him to surgery, he was officially my patient.

I unwrapped the bandage from his knee and saw the damage. His wound needed cleaning, so I injected him with about 25 milligrams of Demerol to ease the pain and broke out the sterile surgical kit. After cleaning the wound and getting him bandaged up again, it was a short gurney ride up to X-ray to get a few shots to help the orthopedic surgeons do *their* job. After X-ray, I checked to see if there were any Marine patients in pre-op. Having a wounded Marine lying next to a wounded NVA soldier, one who may or may not have injured or killed a fellow Marine, was not going to happen in our triage unit. Ever.

We then transported the POW on his gurney to an empty pre-op room where he awaited surgery. I established a superficial relationship with the young man I will call Tranh—made him comfortable, gave him some water to drink, all the usual stuff I'd do for any patient. And then I went to the bathroom to take a pee.

When I returned, I saw one of the corpsman standing over Tranh. He grabbed Tranh's bandaged knee and shook it. "How's that feel, gook!" he said.

Enemy by Michael Sadler

Tranh cried out in pain.

I walked over and pushed my way between the corpsman and Tranh. "If you so much as lay another finger on this wounded soldier," I said to the corpsman, emphasizing the word "soldier" and furious but trying to remain calm, "you will answer for charges of prisoner torture at your court martial."

His response was: "Soldier? That fucking slopehead probably killed some of our guys!"

Maybe, maybe not. But at that moment, I had more respect for Tranh than for a bully and coward who would do such a thing to a helpless individual.

This incident did not make me Mr. Popular with some of my fellow corpsman, but I wasn't entered into a popularity contest—I had a job to do, and a moral responsibility, as well, to provide the best medical care I could muster to anyone—anyone—who needed it. I have often wondered if my corpsman colleague later regaled family, friends, or even total strangers about his brave confrontation with a wounded enemy soldier. Or if, instead, his act of cowardice haunts him to this day. Maybe it's both.

I knew it would be at least half an hour, maybe more, before Tranh's surgery, and a question popped into my head: How often do you get to talk to a prisoner of war? I wasn't a writer then, but something at the time told me this might prove interesting later.

Well, it's 42 years later.

I quickly called for a translator, and the guy showed up within a few minutes. I made it clear to both the translator and Tranh that I was not trying to interrogate Tranh, but rather wanted to know some of his personal background.

The translator relayed what I said, and Tranh looked at me for a long moment, perhaps weighing his options, and then nodded approval. So, for the next twenty or thirty minutes, I had a conversation with a real-life prisoner of war.

Tranh was a junior at Hanoi University when the army came calling for his services. Majoring in mathematics, he told them he would like to graduate the following year. But they would have none of that, even threatening his family if he refused. I didn't ask about the specifics of the threat, but I can conjure up a scenario where refusal is not an option.

Now I'm the kind of person who usually takes people at their word, but just to verify that Tranh was telling me the truth—at least about one thing he said—I took out a pen and drew a triangle on a piece of paper. I marked each of the triangle sides "a" and "b" respectively, and then marked a "c" along the hypotenuse. I wrote underneath: a-squared plus b-squared equals...? What? Since math is all about symbols, it doesn't matter which ones I used—English or Vietnamese. An alien from another galaxy with a basic knowledge of math would know this one.

Tranh looked at the diagram, then at me, and gave me a hint of a dismissive smile. I smiled back. We both knew I was testing him. He quickly filled in the answer: c-squared. It wasn't proof-positive that everything he told me was the truth, but since he had no reason to lie, I think he was being truthful.

Tranh joined the North Vietnamese Army, but he and his fellow soldiers were not given proper training. Or equipment. After only three days practicing with a stick for a rifle, he was sent south with his unit. On his first day south of the DMZ, Tranh got his kneecap shot up. And he was captured. And he was sent to the Da Nang Hospital for treatment. And it was then up to me to ensure he received it.

If Tranh and I were face-to-face out in the bush and in a firefight, there's no doubt we'd both want to kill each other. But in the abstract, I had to ask myself at the time: Was this soldier laying here in this hospital really my enemy?

Prior to joining the Navy, I was a student at Valley College, trying my utmost to NOT go to Vietnam, so I ended up enlisting rather than take a chance on getting drafted into the army. I wanted to be a hospital corpsman, and after passing a battery of tests in boot camp, I trained hard for that job. As it turned out, I went to Vietnam, anyway. Best laid plans of mice and men...

At the time of my conversation with POW Tranh, it sure showed up like two former college students talking to each other, trying to survive a war where all of us were mere pawns in a much larger game—one that cost 58,000 American lives and only God knows how many on their side.

It's a given of warfare that you've got to find something to hate about your enemy; otherwise, it's tough to build up enough piss and vinegar to justify killing him without a second thought.

But for the life of me, I couldn't at the time, or even now, find anything to hate about Tranh.

12

Protagonist
by Jeffrey Alan Rochlin

Sentenced to solitary confinement
wrapped in a strait-jacket of blood
festered wounds weep
from wrist and ankle restraints
Putrefied flesh
permeates the stale humidity
Out of the darkness
a symphony of screams
punctuate gunshot laden nights
At dawn a bullet riddled ballet
staggers through the body spasm Babylon
on a ward of 9 x 12 torture chambers
at Fort Conscience

Skeletons in army nurse uniforms
make rounds
boney fingers pinch noses
slack jaws open wide
They pour rainbows in paper cups
down the throats of spittle-mouth catatonics
Swallow daylight that's an order the nurses grunt
chatter of teeth against clack of jawbone
reverberates up and down the hallway

Returning Soldiers Speak

Osmotic pressure
forces psychotropic toxoids
through semi-permeable membranes
into the brainpan of shell-shocked schizophrenics
harnessed heads decapitate from shackled shoulders
like frozen death sculptures in sleep induced comas
the last protagonists of the apocalypse
are trapped like rats
in a fiery maze of carnage dreamscape

war winds down
troops travel homeward,
nobody comes back.

13

Fear
by Michael Sadler

As a Navy Hospital Corpsman, I worked Triage at Da Nang Hospital in 1969. Triage is the French word for the sorting and handling of casualties, according to certain survivability criteria given the availability of human and technical resources.

Me and my fellow corpsmen treated U.S. Marines arriving from the field of battle in various states of injury, from minor frag wounds to one case of a Marine who lost both legs and his right arm. It was a job I wanted—and got. It was the best job at the hospital, but also the hardest job, too, and admittedly a bit gruesome. But with it came a lot of personal satisfaction.

With a single duty doctor and no nurses, our 24-on, 24-off shift of 10 corpsman staunched the flow of blood from sundry body holes, stabilized vital signs, ran intravenous fluids, did minor surgery on occasion, humped patients on stretchers up to X-ray, then pre-op, and finally off to surgery. If they got to us alive, they usually stayed that way. We sent very few to the morgue.

If a Marine arrived as one of many injured during a major military operation, and he was unfortunate enough to have a low *relative* probability of survival, and there just wasn't the time or resources available to spend on that one guy... sorry, he was going to die. And who made that decision?

All of us at one time or another, individually or in small groups, depending on what was happening and the time it would take to tend to that single individual. During periods of heavy casualties, I remember making such life-and-death decisions, usually confirmed by the duty doctor, but not always. I was 20 years old at the time.

One day on a thankfully slow evening, a Marine came in all by himself via medevac chopper. He had a severe frontal head wound, but because he was the only guy in Triage at the time, we pulled out all the stops.

A stretcher-bearer and I offloaded him from the belly of the chopper and took him quickly into Triage. He had a big bandage over his forehead, but the blood was still seeping through. When I removed the bandage, I saw a huge gaping hole in his forehead ... and his brains were leaking out. I checked and charted his vital signs, which were surprisingly quite normal, put in an IV, and finally applied gauze and a pressure bandage. We then humped him on his stretcher up the short hill to X-ray.

After taking three shots of his head from different angles, we then waited for the results ... and waited ... and waited. After about ten minutes, an eternity during wartime medical response, my patience ran out—at exactly the same time it did for everyone in X-ray, too. Doctors, X-ray techs, and corpsman bailed, all at once.

I entered the central X-ray viewing room to find out what was going on. Inside was a radiologist, an X-ray tech, and a guy who looked decidedly out of place in his camouflage uniform staring at the X-ray viewer. He was from the bomb squad.

I could see the X-rays up on the screen, and from all three angles was the same hemisphere-shaped object, about two inches or so in diameter, along with a little spring and connecting wires at the base, lodged near the front of the Marine's skull.

As we soon found out from his commanding officer, he happened to be walking about thirty feet in front of a launch tube when it tipped off its tripod and fired. The round hit him square in the forehead.

I stepped up to the viewer, and the bomb squad guy explained the situation: He could see from the spring and wiring that the round had spun enough rotations and traveled far enough to arm itself. But because it hit a relatively soft object—in this case a human skull—it hadn't detonated.

Thinking back to what I'd already done thus far, both in transport and in medical attention, I asked, "What would it take to detonate it?"

"Not much," he replied. It had something to do with the little spring, but my thoughts were elsewhere. I explained in what I remember as a trance that I had just changed the bandage and applied a gauze bandage around the Marine's head under a lot of pressure to keep his brains from falling out.

"You're lucky, doc," the man said, and added with some relief, "and so was everyone else within a hundred feet."

Did I mention that after 361 days in Vietnam, this was my last night in Triage, and that I was due to go home in four days? Well, now you know my mindset at the time. Fear.

Fear by Michael Sadler

We all waited for the young Marine to die on the stretcher in X-ray. Waiting for a human being to die was not an easy thing for me, and for a lot of reasons. First among them was holding in balance concern for a wounded Marine's life, in contrast to concern for my own. The Marine was now an unconscious vegetable, and we all knew it would never be otherwise, despite his having a strong pulse and normal breathing. He was not going to die on his own.

There weren't that many good options. Not to be flippant here, but the old pillow-over-the-face option wasn't available, and not only for moral reasons. The added pressure might set the fucking mortar round off! I suppose someone could have injected him with a lethal dose of strychnine, but that didn't seem right, either. And we couldn't just leave him in the X-ray room for God only knew how long. Casualties were slow at that moment, but it usually didn't last long.

The neurosurgeon came down and volunteered to remove the round. A heroic gesture? Perhaps to him. But for everyone else with a functioning brain, it was a very stupid idea—the only neurosurgeon in the entire region, an anesthesiologist needed to administer the gas, nurses to assist, and fellow corpsmen in the operating room. They would all be a risk. And for what, a Navy commendation medal? The Navy captain who ran the hospital thankfully overruled him.

No, the only option was to get him out of there and let him die in solitude. "Where should we put him?" asked the radiologist. Notice the use of the royal "we"? The radiologist knew very well who'd be transporting that Marine to his destination, and it wasn't going to be him. I could only shake my head in comic disbelief. This was definitely a case of *Ya go home with the one who brung ya*, pure and simple. And I had no thoughts of refusing the task, despite my short-timer status. He was my patient from chopper, through Triage, and into the operating room, and protocol is protocol. Besides, if I refused to do it, someone else would have to take up the slack, and I feared shame and ridicule more than I feared dying.

The bomb squad guy looked at me, *not* the radiologist, and said, "Take him down to Lake Monsoon." Lake Monsoon wasn't really a lake, but rather a huge catch basin at the foot of the hill, currently empty due to a lack of rain.

I returned to the X-ray room and broke the news to the stretcher-bearer. He took it rather well, considering. You will know the definition of the word "careful" if you ever have to do what we did next. As we made our way out of the X-ray facility and into the humid evening air, I focused my fear on only one thing: Do not, under any circumstances, including a rocket attack at this very moment, drop this fucking stretcher!

In the longest and most time-consuming 300-foot walk of my entire life, before or since, there were two competing fears in my head fighting for ascendancy: First, that I would, in my haste to get this thing over, lose my grip, trip or stumble, and drop the stretcher—Kaboom! So I walked verrrrry slowly and verrrrrry carefully down the walkway toward Lake Monsoon. But soon the second fear kicked in: In taking too much time to make the journey with such a load, my muscles would eventually fill to overflowing with lactic acid, start to twitch, and then ultimately fail, resulting in my dropping the stretcher anyway. Kaboom!

I stuck with the tortoise approach: take one small step at a time, one foot in front of other, and deal with everything else later—if there is a later.

I found myself staring with unblinking eyes into another set of unblinking eyes—those of the 19-year old seaman's apprentice across from me, who was walking backwards holding up his end of the stretcher. It wasn't really fear that gripped the both of us but rather the pressing need for caution.

Words weren't necessary, because we were both watching for the exact same thing—an eye twitch, a slight error in movement, a slip of the hand, a stumble, something that would signal, in advance, immediate disaster. But then it dawned on me: If it happens, the explosion will be quick and huge, too late to do anything about. There was really no escape from that live round sitting less than a foot away from my crotch. So, put one foot in front of the other, and take it slow and careful.

With everyone evacuated beyond my sight, we had a clear path down the walkway towards Lake Monsoon. It's the only time in my life I've ever felt, without the need for confirmation, a lot of eyes glued on me. I guess if we had blown it—pardon the pun—they'd all at least have had a good war story to tell.

I had a long time to think on that 300-foot journey, and while my first thoughts were definitely fearful ones, they soon gave way to other thoughts—such as this Marine's life cut short by the collateral damages of war and a family member opening the front door to a man in a Marine uniform bearing very sad news.

And I also remember thinking, *is this how it ends?* After surviving unscathed for this long, and on my last night of duty, being in the wrong place and time—just fucking once?

We carefully made our way across the access road and down the short but steep bank of Lake Monsoon, and then carefully laid the stretcher on the sand. I remember saying a few parting words to the Marine, but that brief moment shows up more like a silent dream than anything else, so I don't remember what I said. We climbed the bank and headed back to Triage. Everyone was very relieved nothing had gone wrong.

Fear by Michael Sadler

And then the chief corpsman came up to me, shook my hand, and said, "Congratulations, Sadler, you're officially off-duty." I shook hands all round and walked back to my barracks for a good night's sleep. The next morning I stayed in the barracks while the guys from the bomb squad sandbagged the still technically alive Marine's shoulders, and blew his head off. Later, I heard several guys who witnessed the detonation talking about how it was all "so cool!" For me, it wasn't.

Four days later, on February 28, 1970, now officially an adult at 21 years old, and still in possession of my crotch, plus all my fingers and toes, I got on a plane and flew back to California. And forty years later, I remember it all like it happened yesterday.

14

Midnight
by R. S. Carlson

Dropping my books, I tour the drowsing house,
close the drapes,
turn down the heat,
and pick up the teddy bear,
the one-eyed cat,
the teething ring
and the yellow musical mouse
you pushed through the playpen bars
this afternoon.

I ease into your room
for the midnight check:
the flooring creaks;
the curtains diffuse
the moon-and-streetlamp glare.

In dim shadows
I stand and watch you sleep.
My days are headlined
with anger, argument and riot:
no one lives innocent of war

but you scarcely sigh in your sleep;
clutching your quilt like the future,
your fist holds a dream secure.

15

Slam It Baby
by Gary Champagne

The bases were loaded with one out and I was stepping up to the plate. The score was Us two and Them zero. On the mound was a friend, and playing second base for Them was also a friend. Them came into our house undefeated and on a ten game winning streak. Us was in the bottom half of the division and had yet to turn the season around (we were perennial contenders). I looked into the pitcher's eyes as I stepped into the box. What was going on in his mind? What was he thinking about? What or how to pitch me? I sensed a little fear, or was I reading too much into his movements. He slowly stepped to the rubber and leaned over to get the signal from the catcher. The thought of hitting a grand slam entered my mind, but I knew that by trying, I would most likely not hit one. So I focused on making good contact and trying to get a base hit. The pitcher began his windup and threw a fastball high and outside. Was he pitching me away on purpose? Was he afraid to throw something good or too good to hit? I got back into my batting stance and awaited the next pitch.

The pitcher leans over for the signal. He nods and begins the windup. It's another fastball, but this time it is going over the outside part of home plate waist high. I start my swing and as I am about to hit the ball I close my eyes. The sound of the bat hitting the ball is like an explosion. I feel nothing and only hear the sound. I look up and watch the ball sail over the second baseman's head. Without moving he stares straight ahead. The center fielder and right fielder don't make a move toward the ball either and watch it sail over the right center field wall about twenty feet. As I begin to trot around the bases, the feeling of elation begins to well up inside. My heart begins to pick up steam and the excitement begins to build. As I pass the first base-man, he kicks the dirt in disgust and turns his back. Crossing first base is like receiving a nice sensuous kiss. As I pass the second baseman, he turns away like a spurned lost love. Crossing second base increases the excitement as if I am playing and sucking on a pair of firm breasts. As I approach third, the anticipation keeps building as the shortstop and third baseman have looks of shock and disbelief.

Crossing third base felt like a pussy's warm wet hug. The final trot home was slow and deliberate to increase tension and excitement as the team wait-ed in anticipation. As I Crossed the home plate, the team, the fans and I erupted into a total ecstasy.

no way

16

Rock of Ages
by Kenneth Klemm

I served in the United States Navy from 1984 to 1989, and from 1986 to 1989, I served aboard the guided missile destroyer U.S. Claude V. Ricketts (DDG-5), homeported in Norfolk, Va. In those days, an enlisted man assigned to the fleet had to serve a period of time, 90 days, on the mess decks (the chow line aboard a ship), and my turn came in mid-July of 1987. Our name for that duty was mess cranking.

Navy cooks, at least at that time, were known as Mess Specialists, which seemed pretty appropriate given some of the stuff I was looking at. I guess Ptomaine Slinger was already taken. Anyway, during the period of mess duty, the sailor is detached from his own division and is exclusively assigned to the MS's.

The duties involved carrying boxes and crates of food from the reefer decks to the mess decks, helping set up the dining area for the voracious crew, cleaning the pots, pans and silverware used by both cooks and crew, and cleaning the areas in between meals. There were different areas to be assigned and it was done, at least by our cooks, on a daily basis, so that no one burned out on one particular job.

My ship was assigned to a Mediterranean cruise for our deployment, from October of 1987 to April of 1988, and for the first part of the cruise I would be finishing my tour of duty on the mess decks. I couldn't wait to get back to my group, Anti-Submarine (A/S) division, because I was a Sonar Technician and I felt, and still do, that looking for submarines is a hell of a lot more interesting and challenging than slinging what passed for hash on our mess decks, otherwise known as the scene of the crime.

One of the areas of specialty during the mess tour was the deep sink, a large stainless steel tub in which water is superheated to 180 degrees. It is used to scrub clean the large serving trays and pots and pans used by the Mess Specialists to create their own particular brand of magic. It is hot, dirty and sweaty work, but it isn't too bad because it is solitary, so you get a break from being around hundreds of dudes on a ship only 400 feet long. And it was while I was assigned to the deep sink one morning during our Med Cruise that I was able to see one of the most spectacular sights of my life.

Other than Tijuana, which really shouldn't count, I had never been out of the United States before, and I was really looking forward to seeing France, Italy, Spain, Egypt, Israel and Turkey, where we were scheduled for port visits. Finally, instead of cleaning out toilets, and slinging hash, I was actually going to see the world.

I hated getting up at 4 a.m. each and every morning during the mess duty, and that was another reason I couldn't wait to get back to my own division. On this particular day, I went through the groggy wakeup, feeling hung over even though I hadn't had a beer in three weeks, and then speedily took my shower and got dressed, reporting to the mess decks in time to be assigned to the deep sink.

Even though it was hot and sweaty, I was able to get some quality time to myself and could get a break now and again, because the ravenous crew went through their trays much quicker, and more constantly than they went through the large serving trays. So the guys in the scullery were pretty much busy from start to finish of a meal, whereas I was able to take a break now and again.

I had just finished scouring who knew what (and it was best not to ask too many questions) from the bottom of pan, and set it in the drying rack, when I decided I needed some fresh morning air. We were in the midst of breakfast, and it was around 6:30 or so. So I stepped out onto the main deck to get some cool air. And cool it was. Mid October in the Atlantic is a bit nippy, but it was just what I needed. And I got there just in time to take in a sight that took my breath away.

To the ship's port (left to most people), I was looking at the pink-tinged rays of the early morning sun striking the top of the Rock of Gibraltar. Wow. I had read about that famed rock and fortress in many history books. That was a sight that Nelson had seen on his way to a date with destiny at Trafalgar. It was a sight countless mariners over the centuries had seen, powerful, majestic, projecting power and strength. The Rock of Gibraltar, standing in front of me, so close I could touch it.

I was awed, struck silent by the powerful majesty of that projection as the ship knifed through the cold waters at 20 knots. I stood there, letting the cold wind rush over me, as the Rock slowly faded from view as we headed towards the Mediterranean. What other sights would I see on this cruise? The Mediterranean is a sea of history, both above and below. There were ancient worlds, and cultures to be seen and experienced and for the first time in my Navy career, I was truly excited about what lay ahead.

I don't recall how long I stood there, but it was long enough to watch the Rock recede from sight, though not from memory, as the ship continued steaming ahead with a single-minded purpose.

The Rock towered in my memory as I returned to my chores, but now I felt less like Cinderfella and more like a sailor in the United States Navy on a cruise to show the flag around the world. Now I eagerly looked forward to what the next few months would bring. Seeing the Rock of Gibraltar had given me a physical glimpse at an icon of history and it has left me with a sense of awe that has never faded.

V N Cambodia

17

Another Country Out In the Rain
by Ethan E. Rocke

The Americans scattered like camouflaged ants as the gray, Cambodia sky began spewing swaths of rain. The local villagers slowly disbursed, some of them taking up shelter under umbrellas or awnings with the Marines and sailors. As we stood there waiting for Mother Nature to finish flexing, we stared out at the Islamic Center's large, grass square, now transforming into many mighty lakes and rivers. In the center stood a scrawny little boy, about nine, wearing a pair of oversized shorts and nothing else. He had walked out from the shelter of the mosque across from the classrooms' overhangs, under which most of us were standing, and centered himself like a stage performer where the biggest puddle was quickly forming. He stood there for a moment treelike, absorbing all nature's aggression with a smile. I was so fascinated by him, I almost forgot to pick up the camera around my neck and make some pictures of what I was seeing. The water poured over him as he slowly knelt, prostrating in a way resembling the Islamic prayer posture. He sat on his feet, leaning forward, head hanging down and hands flat on the ground beneath about four inches of water. It was like he was worshiping the water and every feeling it elicited in him. He stood up and began dancing and flailing around, kicking and splashing like a city kid around a summer fire hydrant. Finally, two other children joined him, and the game began. They chased and hurled water at each other with sweeping kicks at the endless puddles beneath them. This went on as long as the heavy rain did, which was for some time.

It was the last day of a two-week civil assistance mission in Cambodia's remote southern farmlands. A Marine correspondent, I deployed there with a detachment from the Okinawa-based III Marine Expeditionary Force. We were there to complete several renovations at a local Islamic center while our Navy brethren provided medical and dental care to the villagers. The mission's purpose was to extend America's hand of charity to the Cham people—Cambodia's small, ethnic-minority Muslim population. It was no coincidence that our gesture of brotherly love was directed at this rather obscure group of poor Cambodians. America's "Long War" was in full step, and we were there to win Cham hearts and minds before any radical Islamists could. The U.S. State Department had recently ramped up its spending in Cambodia, and I couldn't help but notice that the rise seemed to coincide with the country's newfound oil wealth.

In my relatively modest travels as a member of the American military, there is always one constant: the people we encounter on our missions—be it combat, peacekeeping or humanitarian operations—have far less than we do. In fact, most of them subsist at a standard of living that is unfathomable to average Americans. Why shouldn't it be after all? As a child, my world constituted a southern California suburban landscape, timed sprinkler systems coming alive every day to replenish each household's rectangular lot in a mechanical, ordered fashion. Our most prized crop was grass. On hot days, my friends and I would play in the sprinklers, just like the Cambodian kids in the rain. Sometimes, my parents would turn the sprinklers on just for us to run around in them. When it rained, however, we always stayed inside, often pouting and wishing it would stop. Water flowed at our behest from faucets and plastic sprouts in the ground. When it came from the sky, it was a nuisance.

Indoors, there was always a television with its constant strobe of advertisements, reminding us that food came in a wide variety of colorful boxes that lay just on the other side of a successful nagging fit at the grocery store. It was there in middle-class suburbia that my American constant was born: The need for more. More toys. More Fruit Loops. More new clothes. More iPods. More money. More cars. More gas. Just more—always more.

I grew up in the 80s when Cambodia was a country trying to claw its way out of ruin. The Cambodian people had suffered some of the most despicable atrocities of the 20th century under the savage persecution of Pol Pot's Khmer Rouge. It's estimated that the regime was responsible for the deaths of 1.5 million Cambodians, about one fifth of the population. One of the regime's mottoes was "To keep you is no benefit. To destroy you is no loss." They stayed true to that belief, torturing, executing, starving, and enslaving Cambodians on a massive scale in the name of agrarian communism. When I was sent there in August 2007, I saw a wholly different Cambodia than the war-torn country I had heard about in films and television news. Everywhere I went, the people smiled. In the city or in the country, they seemed to be grateful for the relative peace that had finally settled there.

Another Country Out In the Rain by Ethan E. Rocke

I spent a day on a photo expedition with the two human-intelligence Marines from the detachment. We visited the local markets and explored the countryside and its endless rice paddies. I rolled my $120 jeans up to my knees before stepping into one of the paddies. As I was stepping in, one of the intel Marines was stepping out of the foot or so of muddy water. He had been in there for about two minutes, and he discovered a leech on his leg upon exiting. Our interpreter explained that leeches were common in the paddies. I was very uncomfortable with the thought of one of the alien parasites latching itself to my leg. Nevertheless, the best shots were out in the middle of the paddy, and I had to get them. I thought about all those brilliant National Geographic photos and the pain and discomfort the photographers had to brave to deliver them to my pristine world. On top of that, I was a U.S. Marine. How could I fear a measly, little leech? After all, Cambodian men and women spent whole days in the paddies harvesting rice, completely unfazed. I had to go. As I approached with my camera, the farmers smiled and went on toiling in the humid afternoon sun. I spent about ten minutes getting the shots. Then, having avoided contact with the paddy's ghastly little unseen beasts, I hurried back to comfort.

We stayed in rather ironic accommodations while we were there. Our Cambodian base was a five-star beach resort on the Gulf of Thailand about thirty miles west of the Islamic center and the country villagers we were there to help. How a detachment of U.S. Marines ended up with such opulent billeting in a poor, foreign country is beyond me. The benefits of a Republican administration, I suppose.

We made the 45-minute bus ride from the resort to the Islamic center every morning, and every day, we joked and cracked wise to each other about something pertaining to the local villagers' unfamiliar way of life: the ragged clothes they wore, the broken-down shanties they lived in, the flimsy sandals that did little to protect their feet from the mud and feces left by the gaunt livestock that grazed in the center's square.

It probably seems insensitive to make light of the situation in places like Cambodia, but it's the only way to avoid getting caught up in the deep sadness of it all. After all, that's how most of us in America live our lives every day, constantly averting our eyes and redirecting our focus inward. Our leeches live in the world's muddy waters, and we dare not tread there. America's clear water comes from faucets and plastic sprouts in the ground. That's why on a warm, rainy day in America, you're not likely to find any children outside in the downpour, worshipping the rain.

80

18

The Pan Child
by Amy Feemster

I can best nurture my will to create by being free within my mind and speech. In the mind's eye freedom is real. The wind in the willow tree reminds me of the force and fury of my inner being and how the symphony of wind in tree frond leaves bends and sways an orchestra of silence unseen motion. Moving without words, bending without sound, feeling the breeze caress my face, I fly in my mind's eye. I am always flying. God's wings I do not bind, for they remind me that this time here is fleeting and he will call me back to creation someday. And the flying will be hard fought and the winds of creation fierce.

I will also remember a day at Kitty Hawk when I taught Pan to fly, arms outstretched and feet firmly planted. The child of four so small and at a loss of Mother, she took to the wind with eyes closed. Then to the day the Pan child took to ocean with no ship, but just a borrowed mother's mast as she fought the waves. The Pan child rode the ocean and the borrowed mother, felt strength for the little one. And when the Pan child took the light of creation from the sprouting avocado seed, the woman she knew, she knew this one would survive.

Each kneading of bread was the last breath for the time with the lost child was precious and short. Such hurt. Her little head conked out against the window coming home from the beach. The lil' chil'.

When I have a hard day, I remember to step like this little one. I look about and see coal-fire in my heart and eye. Hell I keep banked within me. I will create no more from my womb. My children have grown and gone away. Now I find, I am the Pan child in the wind, I fly in my mind's eye. The birds remind me to dig the soil as they hop instead of flying. "Spring is coming farm girl," they say. I will create a garden in my mind and till the soil. The water will be tears that no longer fall in my quiet, and in my tempest, the rain.

Melissa Mooney was 28 years old in 1999, I was the borrowed mommy. My kids had gone back to their father and Roger had moved in. His daughter was Samantha. She was a little tike that tore my heart and made me feel again. After shutting my heart to all for loss of my children, I could not bear to look at a child. This little one was as fiery as her mother when she would argue with Roger then tear out in her car and I and Sammy would watch as her father Roger would race after her. They were a pair and loved each other greatly. It is a good yet painful memory. Thank you for allowing me to feel.

19

Hard Time
by Dick Howell

Memories... dominate my conscious thought filling the void of emptiness that is the present because nothing is there. And the future, so far off in the distance it can't be seen because the empty void of the present extends far into it, leaving only the past with all the sadness for all my losses, failures, heart breaks and lesser disappointments. Even the good times, are overwhelmed by the pain that inevitably follows. The broken dreams and promises, failed hopes and shattered expectations—all leading to the present. The void that sucks up the past and vomits out the constant, ever present awareness of my wasted life.

Time... that most valued of all human wealth, the illusive quantity of which can only be measured by the occurrence of events or the symbolic attachment of numbers. Like the proverbial watched pot that never boils, it appears to stand still; one day undistinguished from those passed or the ones approaching but for lack of an identifying event. Every minute, hour, day, month, ever so slowly turning to years. Missing. Lost. Ultimately measured by time, the years of incarceration subtract the finite years of my life. Constantly reminded by the conscious mind, this awareness even when sufficiently distracted, the distant powerful throbbing from the subconscious screams the morbid reminder.

Death... stands watching over doing time, waits impatiently, emanating a feeling of dread. I experience a dying of spiritual consciousness, barely aware of a living world but far removed, physically, mentally, with only a bare thread of an ability to observe and hear that life does go on... elsewhere.

The constant aching, pain, thoughts of loved ones, needing and being needed but deprived by some fabricated barrier creating a form of death, however temporary or artificial.

Sleep... that nebulous state so often seen as something similar to death becomes welcomed, craved, cherished, prolonged, offering me the only remnant of peace, freedom, happiness... living. It pours forth in dreams—lengthy, elaborate and relished by the dreamer. Only sleep offers a too brief respite from the dull monotonous agony. Sleep, which is normally avoided, minimized or taken as a grudging payment for the privilege of good health and an active life. Always knowing that in the distance wakefulness awaits a return to my stagnant death-like state of imprisoned existence.

Thai Soup

Thai Soup

20

Thai Soup
by Ethan E. Rocke

Symmetrically sliced mushrooms perform
Like synchronized swimmers
In a steamy pool
Of hazy-orange shimmer.
Swirling Cilantro stalks draw
Yin Yang symbols in a pool of perfect Zen,
That breathes life into conflicted spirits.
They fly up my nose; rush to the back of my brain.

I close my eyes and inhale
The smell of onion and lemongrass,
Galanga-Kha and fish sauce.
I see across the Pacific …

I see the steamy raunch of Walking Street.
Pattaya Beach. Vegas on crack.
How to market human trafficking:
"Good guys go to heaven; bad guys go to Pattaya"
I exhale the pungent sea air
Mingling with piss and prostitutes
On grimy, littered streets
Where babies grow up to be bar girls,
Like the ones we're hunting tonight.

Returning Soldiers Speak

I'm full on Thai soup and ready
For the main course
Of alcohol and virgin girls
In pink baby-doll dresses
And no panties. Mirrored tables
And low bar fines. Affordable virgins;
More brilliant marketing.
Keep the drinks coming and save the stories
About your family, hun—
How they sent you to the city
To make it big as an ornament
During this annual American exercise
Of diplomatic debauchery—
Economic stimulus by way of
Physical stimulus.

Marines and sailors do their part
To fuck the American dream Into Thailand,
One sacrificial farm girl at a time.
The lucky girls attach like crabs
To the marrying types,
The Ugly Americans
Who want a repeat performance
Forever, and are willing to pay
All the way home.
(Like Pretty Woman but sadder.)

I smell the soup steaming up, and
It's the leathery-skinned Euro troll,
His sloppy Hawaiian shirt and ladyboy pet.
The bar with the endless naked girls,
Dancing on glass ceilings,
Going down on each other
In an empty hot tub in the floor.
Sex as performance and
The pleasure-mongers barely notice.
Bar girls in their laps.

It's the Tom Yum! Soup,
The one that leaves a burn when it bites you,
Like the place that it came from, where
The soul often insights you

Thai Soup by Ethan E. Rocke

About things you didn't know
Were swirling around inside you,
Like that spicy bowl of Zen
That tastes more dark than light
And worries my western mind
With the thought that maybe I am too—
More dark than light—
If I love the hot and sour
Experience of
Thai soup.

21

Brushstrokes from Hell
by Jim Terpstra

I didn't like studying in high school, which made me figure college wouldn't be a good idea. So, I signed up for the Navy when I was a senior in high school and made my parents proud. The ironic part was the Navy plopped me in school for a year and a half to prep me for a job that I didn't like, and really wasn't good at.

After my training I was transferred to the 6th Fleet Flagship the USS Belknap. Her homeport was on the west coast of Italy in a town called Gaeta. Gaeta is one of those beautiful towns they use in paintings … so much history, a great beach … and all the locals couldn't stand us.

I don't blame them, 500 testosterone-crazed American sailors in their 20s and 30s terrorizing their town and their women. You could compare it to a never-ending birthday party of 5-year-olds at "Chucky Cheese."

The USS Belknap was basically a taxi for the 3-star admiral to cart him around from country to country in the Mediterranean to do, what I assumed, was political stuff.

We were selected as one of the first American ships to visit the USSR in years. Our division helped paint the outside of the ship for the visit. However something political was exploding in Lebanon, so we were ordered to cruise around in little circles off their coast and missed our visit to the Soviet Union.

But we still received a Letter of Appreciation for helping paint.

Next big thing was the Pope's ship. Who knew the Pope had a ship? I didn't know the Pope had a ship. There must be a flood scheduled that I don't know about.

Well, his ship was going to be cruising past us on our starboard side at the range of about a mile. So the starboard side of the ship—and only the starboard side of the ship needed to be painted—and since our division did such a great job last time, we were ordered to help again.

In the end, the Pope wasn't actually on his ship but we received another Letter of Appreciation nonetheless.

The ship's picture was the next time we painted the outside of the ship.

After we were done, some boatswain mate found that if he mixed the paint with some special lacquer, it would shine to a hue that made the captain blush. So, we immediately repainted the ship and received another Letter of Appreciation.

Next was the Malta Summit, where the first President Bush was meeting with Mikhail Gorbachev for some dog and pony show.

We received two things, a special hat and a new paintbrush. But this time it was different because we had to slap paint on both the outside AND the inside of the ship.

Letter of Appreciation #4.

So, that's the highlights of my military experience.

Oh, I also got roofied and raped by my best friend on the ship.

If I reported it, I would have gotten kicked out of the military the same day.

I ate in the same chow hall as him…

I worked right next to him…

And I slept in the same berthing compartment as him for over a year and a half before I could get transferred.

It's ok. I have been trying to murder my feelings of shame and guilt these last 20 years with a lot of booze and weed. Those four Letters of Appreciation were great to roll joints with, because that's all they were good for.

And that year and a half of specialized schooling can be shrunken down to one sentence my Master Chief barked at us: "Looks like you boys are going to learn how to paint."

Well, I'll let you in on a little secret … I already knew how to paint.

22

Soul Dark
by Kenneth Klemm

The darkness, my unfriend, has come to see me once again. Outside my window the day is bright. Inside my cluttered trailer it is dingy and dim. Inside my mind it is dark and cold. A black fog has come rushing in, filling my mind, seeping into my soul. My thoughts get foggy, my vision dims, and now I lie inside a blanket of fear.

Like the clutter in my trailer, the darkness in my mind comes and goes. It is like the ocean's tides, advancing a little further each time, and staying just a little bit longer. The days blend into one another, the next one seemingly beginning even before the current one is done. Like a prisoner in solitary confinement, I have lost track of time.

Some days, the fog lifts and I can taste my mac and cheese and hear the birds singing in the sycamore trees. Some days the black fog rushes in, dimming my sight. My energy drains like milk from a broken carton, and I cannot get out of bed. I lie lost in darkness, unmoving, uncaring, unmindful of what's going on around me.

Some days the fog clears and the whispering of the wind through the treetops fills me with rustling joy. I savor these moments like a condemned man eating his last meal, for I know that they will not last long.

Some days the darkness falls on my soul like the night of a new moon. On these black days, my bed is my prison. All I can do is lie there and hope the fog recedes as rapidly as it came, but it never does. Once it's here, it lingers like in-laws at Thanksgiving dinner, wanting to fill every last space of my soul with its clinging darkness.

The fog has lifted momentarily, and I can hear the gentle tapping of rain on the tin roof. At last, a brief moment of clarity. It brings a smile to my face, a movement unfamiliar to me these days. It is but an illusion, a mirage, a mere fleeting moment of peace, a glimpse of what I could have had but now cannot get. The darkness descends again, occluding my mind, eclipsing my soul, and weighing down my spirit.

I cannot control my body now. Thoughts of movement do not lead to action. I am paralyzed, black chains of despair wrapped tightly around my mind, body and soul. I can do nothing now except to ride out the storm and hope that it passes, leaving me in the light on the other side.

The light. I dream of the light, a beacon to guide me out of this maze of darkness that threatens to strand me in the shadowy valleys. I dream of finding the light, of feeling the warmth of the sun against my skin, of bright beams to chase away the black tendrils of despair wrapping around my mind.

But it is only a dream. I cannot find the light, cannot reach the light, cannot feel the light. The light that I do find is a soulless specter, a ghostly beam devoid of all warmth. That feeble beam is far too weak to penetrate the darkness that tears away at my soul with rending talons.

How long must I endure the repeated incursions of this black cancer slowly eating away at me, tearing at my soul bit by bit? How many days have I spent paralyzed in fear, trapped in my bed unable to get out? I have lost track, one day blending into another, with fewer and fewer beams of light to penetrate the growing wall of darkness that now threatens to totally engulf me within it.

If I give in, if I let it roll over me, through me and take me in its embrace, then all will be lost. I know there will be no coming back from that. And as tired as I am, I am not ready to quit the game just yet.

I can't remember exactly when the blackness first came, but I was in the Navy when it did.

I was on quarterdeck watch in the middle of the night, when the Petty Officer of the Watch pulled his service weapon, an M-1911 Colt .45, and shot himself in the chest. I am pretty sure that is when the darkness first started coming around.

And now, twenty years after my discharge, I am in bed in the middle of the day. I think it is the middle of the day. I can't really tell. I keep the blinds down most of the time now; the bright light of day hurts my eyes. I blink, and the room comes into focus.

At last, the darkness passes. It always does but it always comes back. Each time it is a little bit stronger, a little bit darker. What if it doesn't go away next time? I must fight this, or let the darkness sweep me over the edge and into the abyss of despair. And then I may seek the final solution that my shipmate sought and found so many years ago.

I know that I must fight, but I cannot fight this battle alone. Tired of being tired, afraid of being afraid, I finally muster the strength of the moment and find a phone number I have had in my wallet for several months. It is a Veteran's hotline, and I finally make the call that I should have made when I got the business card. I am tempted to put it off until tomorrow, but I push on and make the call.

I talk to a man named Paul, and before I know it, I have made an appointment to speak to a mental health professional at my local VA hospital. Exhausted but hopeful, I hang up the phone and write the appointment on the back of the card before the black fog comes rushing in once more.

23

Scales
by Terry Mickel

The delicate balance of justice and injustice is played out in our everyday lives but more so in war. When we engage our enemies, whether in combat or otherwise, are those moments judged fairly by us? Most oftentimes during war they are not. We have a single mission in hand and that is to destroy our adversary without hesitation. In the very midst of our decisions in some aspect we have to justify within ourselves that what we are doing is justifiable. So we are able to move on with the task at hand. The injustice can creep into our consciousness if we allow ourselves to be and feel human.

Every decision we make has an unknown effect of justice and injustice. These two principles are closely related but traveling in different directions. Each one of us, when we encounter people, places or things during a stressful event such as combat, every choice we make is one of justice or injustice. Our beliefs and training come into play as we move forward with the objective that was assigned to us.

There has to be a certain amount of belief in what we are trained to do whether we like it or not.

War is an ugly event that carries lifetime effects.

The question of morality weighs heavily on one's mind during wartime, which makes every action we take a one of justice or injustice. The time we spend in combat always plays a role in your life no matter what the outcome. To live every day with a vigor for justice or injustice can stem from the choices we made in war. To strike a balance is a very difficult job to undertake but it's necessary in order to maintain some peace of mind.

Justice or injustice is determined in a single moment when confronted with the enemy. The fear of not making it through in one piece has a major impact on that decision of justice or injustice. Some of us rationalize what we did in combat in order to survive another day. There are many ways of dealing with making such a profound decision under this stressful event. So many factors come in to play and impact our actions and the actions of others around us. In some ways we are all affected by justices or injustices. Finding the balance of these principles in combat is a very tricky and delicate matter.

Each one of us has a scale within us that usually leans one way or the other. Depending on which way the scale is tilted will influence our decision of justice or injustice.

24

The T-Shirt
by R. S. Carlson

For some trips
the memories swell from
paging back through the albums
smelling of plastic,
and 4x6 prints
sticking in their sleeves.

Certain views
still tug at the ribcage-
the shades of gray reporting the grandparents' 1886 marriage,
and blurred great grandparents' Dakota territory homestead dugout
the red carp swarming for feed in a Sung Dynasty pond
the gold-leafed spire of a Lao wat at sunset,

But some pictures
never leave the neural net,
and some nights, dreams keep too clear
the New Year's party for kids
at the hospital for the blind
that serves recent survivors of the last war's old munitions:

the five-year-old fingers I guide
to the popcorn in the bowl I hold
belong to thin arms bracketing a powder-blue T-shirt
with a pink Teddy Bear beaming me a snide smirk
as it strides over the legend
Mine Test.

25

Remembering War
by Jeffrey Alan Rochlin

Face to face I killed human beings for my country
I killed humanism for my country, I shot humanity point blank
I killed human kind to survive and killed myself in the process
Family reunions are ghost gatherings because of me

My American dream is a nightmare of atrocities
writhing in a wet sheet coffin
I lay inside exploding battlefields
curled up in a flesh foxhole
crunch of bone in my ear spray of blood in my face
overhead body parts and shrapnel fly through the air
in a macabre slaughterhouse of mutilated army men

I fear sleep, I fear cognition
Jack boots of a million corpses
march in lock step through my brain
(cadence caller's chant) *US Army Robbed My Youth*
Uncle Sam Got a New Gold Tooth
On his left.....on his left.....on his left right left

one by one a million corpses gnaw on my conscience
I have nothing left to sacrifice the hunger never stops
I could put a bullet in my brain
demons would

just chew it up
and spit me out

Johnny went off to war
He came back in a test tube
a couple of stains of DNA
are all that's left of his remains
Cause of death on his VA form
stamped, not combat related
They buried Johnny in a shot glass
Nobody recognized him at the funeral

Sara Jane went off to war
depleted uranium runs through her veins
Gave birth to a cyclops
The VA said her ovaries were not to blame
Mother and child are victims
of armor piercing weapons technology
Locked away from scrutiny
in a padded cell asylum

The biosphere is black and blue and bleeding
Death mucks up the atmosphere
Gunpowder plumage decorates the countryside

Vietnam veterans
homeless madmen at suicide central
trapped inside toxicosis-infested mind fields
Watching "Faces of Death" slide shows
in body parts boutiques with napalm fireworks
low crawling through insect infirmaries
kissing dirt under booby trapped barbed wire
inch by blood-stained inch
through carnivals of carnage
in neighborhood jungles of America
Vietnam Veterans got spit on

Now I lay me down to die
in rows of body bags planted by geometricians
The perfectness of each headstone
lined up in formation as far as the eye can see
Insignia of faith two-crossed $1.98 cent American flags

Remembering War by Jeffrey Alan Rochlin

The sameness of each whitewashed marker dressed up for Memorial Day
cast stoic shadows on the death march of loved ones
Name Rank & Serial Number
Row 19 Plot 32
Rochlin, Jeffrey A.
Medic Specialist 4th Class
US56718963 Jewish

Let's toast to my debauchery
chase away this destiny
Oh God please let the
alcohol slow down this
sanguineness centrifuge
spinning in my head
let's raise our glasses
shoot one more down for God
shoot one more down for country
shoot one more down for every disembodied
veteran haunted by visions of disemboweled bodies
inside scavenger ravaged backyard battlegrounds
Once you taste death every face every name every
family you displace lingers on every breath taken
Death scenes of soldiers who fertilize the earth
played out in theaters of war run nonstop
at the cine-a-plex inside your head
In the loneliness of nighttime
In the darkness of the hour
inside the devil's lair
insomniac philosophers
zen masters of pain
sit in a catatonic lotus
inside a barbed wire pentagram
battling demonologists
on the outskirts of insanity
in a backroom of my brain
locked and loaded in
a life & death struggle
the chrome plated barrel
lays heavy
in the salvia
on my tongue
my conscience

on the trigger
flames of damnation
lick my naked flesh
desecration angels
swirl about my neck
and shoulders
ball peen hammer
cold anvil craniotomy
strapped to a mortician's slab
in the temple of morbidity
remembering war

26

A Soldier's Tale
by Terry Mickel

I believe we are born with a clean slate and are unaware of the beautiful and bad things that surround us. Throughout high school I was a normal teenager with high hopes and big dreams. I was sociable, had a lot of friends and was close to my family. I got good grades and during my senior year worked at a 7-Eleven to help pay for my graduation. And I liked the ladies a lot, too. I was vibrant and full of life.

Before I graduated I joined the army at the tender age of 17. I wanted to go to college so that's why I enlisted. Coming from a very small town in the great state of Mississippi, totally naive to the world, I was exposed to many things good and bad. As a member of the 101st Airborne, I had to grow up fast.

Then the war happened. Iraq invaded Kuwait. I received word that I was going to combat. My life changed in that moment. I became overwhelmed with fear and anger for having to go. I had no idea what to expect or even if I would return home alive or in one piece. That's a very sobering thought. It's a feeling that I do not ever want to experience again.

Our mission was to cut off and kill the enemy to prevent them from returning to Baghdad and setting up defensive positions over the highway and across the desert between Basra and Baghdad. As we were en route to our position there was a lot of carnage along the way. I had never seen a dead body before that was burned beyond recognition. In that moment the reality of human existence set in. I often wonder who were those people and the effect their loss must have had on their families.

I also realized that could be me. I couldn't and didn't want to believe what my eyes had seen and the emotions that came along with it. There was a sense of sadness and guilt for what had happened to those Iraqi soldiers. After all, they were human, too.

I can still see those images to this very day and I will probably carry them with me for the rest of my time here on this earth. I use that reality-check to remind me how valuable and precious life really is and to always remain grateful.

The entire time I was in the war I felt alone with a sadness mixed with fear and anger. I was mad at the world for putting me in this horrible position. As a scared teenager, I just wanted to go home. The sergeant I was attached to and I did not get along. We got into verbal and physical altercations out in the desert and I felt he might kill me then blame it on the enemy combatants. I feel he was a racist; his words gave him away. I felt surrounded by the enemy. I always was on guard out of fear for my safety. I felt like I was in constant danger.

So after returning home from the war, I was not that happy-go-lucky enthusiastic kid anymore. That all disappeared and had been taken away from me. I was very angry, guarded and sad. I was unable to sleep because of the terrible images of the dead and burned bodies I saw in Iraq. I was paranoid of everything and everybody and had to protect myself at all times. These were feelings I never felt before I went to combat, so a lot of times I didn't know how to deal with them. They were strong and overwhelming at times. I lost my desire for the things I liked before such as football, basketball and being around people. I became increasingly isolated, angry and wondered why I had to go to war. I didn't understand how or why this was happening to me.

My family had no clue what was taking place nor could they have understood. I was home yet felt alone again. My folks were afraid of me and noticed the changes that had and were taking place. I would cry for no reason and became angry over the smallest things.

I have had much difficulty in my life with family, maintaining friendships, romantic relationships, housing and keeping a steady job. My life has been negatively impacted by my time in the military. It's extremely difficult for me to trust anyone or to let my guard down. And yet there are good things that came from my time in the army, like discipline, order, integrity, honor and mental toughness.

I like the person I've become so therefore I wouldn't change having gone to war nor would I do it again.

27

An Innocent Man is Hard to Find
by James Mathers

The priest told him that he was born guilty and must atone by being a good boy. He told his mom and she said the old priest was full of it, and that he was innocent and was her "dear heart," and so he ran free and happy in a forest that led to a sandy beach on a remote peninsula on Puget Sound, where he splashed on the warm, morning tide flats, chased seagulls and poked gleeful fingers into clam holes to get the spurt of hot salt water.

Then a red tide came in carrying the flotsam of war, and left it there, up and down his beach as far as he could see. Battered helmets, kapok life preservers, lots of white hats, a boot with a foot in it and soft grey fragments of—what? Fish? Men? Hard to tell after a journey across the Pacific, his dad said. Dad said the dogs of war had been let loose and this was some of the stuff the boy would have to look at, and that it would be a lot worse after the dirty Japs got here.

Everywhere there were new sights and sounds and furies. It was really scary for the boy. Suddenly everybody was gone! Except kids and old people—and mom, but even mom had to go to work every day now at Boeing. The kid wondered if the foot was uncle Bobby's who was in the navy and who left home right after something called Pearl Harbor.

Nana had to take care of him now. Retreat to her warm arms and soft bosom was always a comfort and haven from the thought of the dirty Japs who wanted to shoot his dad and stick a bayonet in his mom.

Then the kid was in third grade and the Japs hadn't shown up and dad came home from the port of embarkation where he worked, and he said that we had killed 350,000 dirty Japs that day. Then the next day he said that we had killed 200,000 more. Everybody jumped up and down and drank too much. Everybody except Nana who said that it was a cruel god who let them kill so many innocent people. The kid knew he was an innocent and he piped up and said that nobody had killed him. Everybody laughed except Nana. She went to see the priest.

Then the kid was an old man looking at the picture of lower Manhattan in flames, the one with the Statue of Liberty standing helplessly by. Hot tears streaked his face and he thought he could make out the tears on her face. He wanted to turn her around. Away from the outside world. She had given quite enough to them. He wanted her to hold up the beacon for us. Then he thought about Nana's cruel god and had no desire to speak to any priest.

The old man thought about the dirty Japs of sixty years ago. They were long gone. In fact he had had tea the year before in Tokyo with an old kamikaze pilot who was ready to take off and crash his plane into a US carrier, but suddenly didn't have to go. Saved by the death of more than half a million women, kids and old people. He had said that he still felt strong guilt. That he still could not bear the pain of that blow. Today, the old man knew what the old kamikaze pilot was talking about. No. He would still not go to the priest.

He thought of the dirty gooks of Korea, the dirty slopes of Vietnam. The dirty ruskies, the dirty commies. Gone. Gone like the dust. He had flown Korean Airlines to the Orient and found a people of quiet elegance and dignity. He had shopped among the open and generous Vietnamese people of Garden Grove. He had partied with Russians whose hearts seemed as big as their magnificent country. He had befriended the ex-commies in San Francisco communes who had decided after rigorous experimentation that collectivism doesn't work—too many cops to make sure that everybody did their chores. They moved their communes to the country with his friend Peter Coyote and became dirty tree-huggers. What else is new he thought?

Suddenly there was the face of the demon! Front page picture. A dirty a-rab, rug headed-cocksucking-motherfucker right next to Two World coming down. Then the president said the dirty a-rabs are coming here to kill us unless we kill them first. But now the boots with feet in them lying on the streets of Baghdad belong to somebody else's uncle Bobby. The rage exploded. The old man ran outside into the night and screamed his guts out—no time now to wonder if he would ever again break bread with some of the most gracious and hospitable people on earth.

The mullahs tell their people that their suffering is the fault of Americans. That to die killing one will get you a ticket to heaven and virgins to fuck for all of eternity. Jerry Falwell tells his following that it's our own fault. That god is punishing us for letting the dirty homos live, and for letting women have a choice. Then a priest in Two World dies administering last rites to a fallen fire fighter.

These damned priests, the old man thought. Either driving their miserable people to some suicidal war, or fanning the fires of hatred and bigotry, or holding up their dead for god to see. Maybe tomorrow he would find one and ask him what the hell they think they're doing. Sure, Nana used to talk to the priest—all the time—but all she knew about was love. Then he thought of the words Will Shakespeare put into Hamlet's mouth: "Now wipe away all the trivial fond records from the table of memory."

Time for his walk. But tonight the old man slipped his beretta into his belt before he stepped out into the darkness.

28

Kentucky Clouds Over The Green-Eyed Monster
by Hugh Martin

-Fort Knox, June 2002

After bear-crawls and overhead arm-claps, we stood in the sawdust pit with Drill Sergeant Irky, who called himself the Green-Eyed Monster. Irky yelled about orders: listening, obeying, following through quickly. As an example, he mentioned Private Henke, who had a clear strand of snot hanging from his left nostril and was breathing hard enough that his head bobbed, as if in approval of everything Irky said. Henke was *A good private*, Irky said, and *He knows how to take orders. Even if I told you to eat this sawdust, Henke, you'd do it, wouldn't you? Yes, Drill Sergeant!* Without pausing, Irky yelled, *Henke, eat sawdust!* No one, not even Irky, thought he'd do it, but Henke looked down at the sawdust, dove to his hands and knees, and scooped a handful to his mouth as if drinking from a stream. Eyes closed, he chewed robotically, a beard of dust stuck to his face. *Henke, you stupid private, spit it out*, Irky said and pulled him up by his shoulder while Henke spit. He ordered us to drink water and we lifted the warm, green canteens from our cargo pockets. Henke swished it around his mouth like Listerine and spit and spit. *Henke, you're a good soldier*, Irky said and patted him on the back, *But don't eat sawdust*. Other orders would arrive: mop the hallway; shine your boots; run two miles; go to Iraq. But for now, Irky told us, we'd move this wall of sandbags to the other side of the pit, where they'd just been moved from the day before.

Great poem

29

God Bless America
by Jeffrey Alan Rochlin

Iraqi dictator "Made in USA" fries in electric chair "Made in China." No bid govt. contractors buy island villas in no extradition tax-free paradise. Uncle Sam swipes his star spangled debit card at the Chinese Export Exchange and bankrupts the country. God bless America!

Veteran's come home in flag draped coffins, dog tags jammed between their teeth, death benefits held hostage by blood money accountants who leverage tax free interest on debt to society for the prophets of profit at War Inc. God bless America.

Tattoos dye out in dead skin dumpsites. Reanimation benefits denied. Medics at Blood Bath & Beyond ship bagged and tagged body parts to home depots for the memorial weekend lowest price guaranteed specials on do it yourself backyard burial equipment. God bless America!

My husband came home from the VA hospital in an envelope. A couple of stains on his mangled dog tags folded into a death certificate.
Staff Sergeant Joseph Madison 1978-2004 God Bless America.

A bar owner from a neighborhood watering hole in Jacksonville sent home to die via ups second day air with bowel and colon cancer poisoned by *depleted uranium* armor on the M1, M1A1, and M1A2 Abram's tanks commandeered on his 3rd tour of duty in Iraq.
Capt. Sergio Diamonte 1976-2005 God Bless America.

Returning Soldiers Speak

Uncle Eddie came home from *Camp Victory* in a test tube wrapped in bubble pack. His family poured Uncle Eddy's remains into silver goblets with tequila shots and drank to his memory. We love you Uncle Eddie, you will always be a part of us as long as we live.
PFC Edward Valez 1987-2006 God Bless America.

Our daughter's remains came home from *Falluja* in a group of flat rate boxes from the post office. On Monday head. On Tuesday torso. On Wednesday extremities. On Thursday two jars one liquefied, one scrambled. On Friday family got together for a wake, raised their glasses eulogized unreasonable fact similes of their baby girl. Saturday buried on her 24th birthday.
Lieutenant Jane Simmons 1983-2007 God Bless America.

American soldiers sent home to die redacted from the death toll non-sequiturs in the spin of propaganda roulette. God Bless America.

Disoriented, veterans with *PTSD*, forage the back streets and alleyways of our cities in search of a way back that doesn't exist. God Bless America.

"Zombie battalions" destined to chase their "organic entities" through eternal damnation. Never Rest In Peace. God Bless America!

You can see right through the spirit of a boy
When you bend him until he breaks. God Bless America.

You can see right through the spirit of a girl
When you bend her until she breaks. God Bless America.

Young soldiers never die they just fade away
In the limbo of lost souls. God Bless America.

30

mode (handwritten annotation)

Dogface Soldier
by William Galloway

This journey started in 2005, about a week after my 20th birthday. It was the first time I had ever been to Los Angeles, and I was there joining the United States Army! I would be lying if I did not say that I felt proud at the time. After the recruitment process they put me up in a hotel for the night somewhere in Los Angeles and flew me out first thing in the morning to "Fort Lost in The Woods," Missouri. I still remember dealing with those bad attitude civilians issuing us our equipment, who used their false sense of authority to fuck with us new soldiers. After that we were rushed onto a bus and dropped off into the waiting arms of our drill sergeants. The red bricked barracks were my new home for the next couple of months.

"Staying under the radar" was not my forte, but my mind was washed all the same. Looking back on what we were taught kind of puts today's military dysfunctions into perspective. Here is an example: "What makes the green grass grow? Blood! Blood! Red red blood!" is what we knew recruits had to repeat over and over as we thrust out bayonets into our invisible enemies. We also sang about killing baby seals as we jogged around the base. Things like that put a young soldier in a certain mentality, War mentality. Good thing we had a "war president" to justify our "war ready" soldiers.

After I completed basic training, I was a bit disappointed. It was not as challenging as I had expected, but I had to start my job training all the same. I signed up to be a heavy construction equipment operator so now I had to learn 5 pieces of earth moving equipment in two to three months. It was interesting to say the least because as soon as I would get the hang of one piece of equipment we would have to start on a new one.

After my training I was placed in a fueling unit and never did one day of heavy construction equipment work. They call that *cross training*. Hot refueling helicopters was much more exciting anyways, I think. Hot refueling is when a helicopter lands with its propellers still spinning so it can immediately take off after we have finished fueling it up. At night you could see the static electricity on the propellers. It was exciting but could also be frightening at times.

Shortly after arriving at my permanent duty station, I was told to pack up and prepare to ship out to Iraq. I was in disbelief at the time because I had just arrived fresh out of basic training and my daughter was just born. I had expected to be able to finally spend some time with my new family. The night before I was supposed to leave I was told, "Never mind. You will be waiting in rear detachment until your unit arrives back from Iraq." So I spent the next couple months on funeral details and welcome back ceremonies. I will never forget the pain on the families' faces during the funerals. I remember the children standing there not really sure what to think while their mommies were given folded flags in place of their daddies, and a ceremonial tree planted in their memory. Some wives would break down, some would try not to, but the pain was clear and present, nonetheless. This was the hardest detail I had to be a part of, not only because of the despair from the families but because of the trees. There was one tree planted for every dead soldier and there were thousands of them. That symbolism can be overwhelming.

One night before some soldiers were getting ready to return state side, I was helping get the ceremony ready for the next day. We were just finishing up an archway made of balloons and I went outside to have a smoke. It was a stormy night. While I was outside smoking I heard a loud bang! It was so loud it echoed through the whole hanger. If you know anything about hangers you know they are huge. Lightning had struck the top of the hanger, bounced to a puddle on the floor inside the hanger, and then struck a soldier standing next to it. He was eventually discharged in the coming months due to injuries.

The day finally came when I was assigned to a unit and the fun started. At first glance my unit sergeant said I was trouble. He said it was just a matter of time until I fucked up. One funny thing I remember was during my first morning of P.T. (physical training) with the unit, we had to sing the *Dogface Soldier* song, which was sung every morning before the unit started exercising, but I knew none of the words so I just stood there mouthing every other word trying to act like I knew what I was singing.

This is the *Dogface Soldier* song: "I wouldn't give a bean to be a fancy pants marine, I'd rather be a dogface soldier like I am. I wouldn't trade my old OD's for all the Navy's Dungarees for I'm the walking pride of Uncle

Dogface Soldier by William Galloway

Sam. On the Army posters that I read it say's be all that you can be so they're tearing me down to build me over again. I'm just a dogface soldier with a rifle on my shoulder and I eat raw meat for breakfast E'V'RY day. So feed me ammunition keep me in the third division your dogface soldier's A-Ok. "

I lived in a house on base with my wife and daughter (who was a baby at the time) but my wife and I argued a lot. Military marriages usually don't last. Mostly because of constant deployment and rushed marriages. Married soldiers get paid more than single soldiers so sometimes people will get married when they are not ready to because of money. We were not ready to get married but we did because of money and both equally suffered the consequences. It got to the point where I was given a direct order from my unit commander to not go to my house and had to live in the barracks.

Eventually I was caught going back to my house and was ordered by the unit sergeant to write a 500 word essay on the importance of following a direct order. Me being the genius I am and already opposing the war, I decided to add, "If George Bush would have followed a direct order 9/11 would have never happened." Needless to say my sergeant did not like that and made me read it in front of the whole platoon and then I was ordered to re-write it with 1,000 words. This is just one of the many times I was paraded in front of my platoon. Humility does not work when you stop giving a fuck.

The wife and I continued to fight until I finally convinced her to move back to California. It turned out to be a double-edged sword. As soon as she left I was out on the town every weekend drinking, smoking weed, taking ecstasy and on top of that madness, I carried a pistol everywhere I went. This was done on a regular basis. And it was all fun, *party-freedom-time* until I got a DUI. Then I was restricted to post, well supposed to be. I had trouble being told what I could and could not do. But regardless of what I did off duty, when I put on that uniform and laced up my boots, I was a good soldier. I followed my orders with a sense of purpose and took pride in my opportunity to serve in the United States Army. I realized I was doing something that most people will never do in their entire lives. What I lacked was discipline. I was being disrespected by some of my superiors, while dealing with personal issues at the same time. By dealing I mean drinking, and in a military-type structure you are trained not to question higher ranks. Everyone deals with that in different ways. I believe that is one of the reasons why there are tragic shootings by soldiers on military bases. I have personally experienced this pressure and abuse by higher ranks and it can make you snap.

I decided to rebel and have an "I don't give a fuck" attitude. I created a bond with a group of similar minded soldiers in my unit and we became a family. After I failed numerous "random drug tests" for marijuana I was sentenced to a short stay at a Navy brig. What was funny to me was, as soon as I was sentenced, myself and another soldier (whom I am keeping anonymous) were immediately put in handcuffs and in my opinion, paraded around base before going to the Military Police Station. We were not allowed to go home and stayed the night at the Military Police Station's jail cells. The next day my stay at the brig was built up to be worse than it really was by the sergeants transporting me, but soon after I arrived it turned out to be more of a vacation from the military, but with bars and cells, than punishment. Same as any jail, I was told when to eat, sleep, and shower.

Shortly after being released back to my unit, I received the news from my unit sergeant that I was going to be discharged and I would not be going to Iraq with the rest of my unit. That news hit my heart like a ton of bricks. I was holding back tears, but what did I expect? If I ever regretted anything in my life, it was that moment. Especially after I was told, "I don't want to go to Iraq without you" by a good friend, followed by his look of disappointment and hurt. I can still feel how it made me feel to this day.

My unit was shipped off shortly after and I was back to where I started, in rear detachment, this time waiting for my discharge. The term "shit soldier" is a universal term that would be used for a soldier like I was at the time and I sure felt like it. For a long time after I was fully discharged I was glued to the news every time the word Iraq was mentioned, still mentally beating myself up with meaningless thoughts like, What if something happens to someone and maybe if I were there I could have saved them? Eventually two years went by and everyone made it back safely. This part of my life taught me that my selfish actions do not always affect just me; they also affect the dogface soldiers.

31

Combat Photographer
by Ethan E. Rocke

*-For Stacy Pearsall and all the shooters who have seen what can never be
unseen*

A shutter click in combat is deafening.
Light and shadow—boxed up like muted souls—
Cheap imitations of what once was.
Click-open—Click-close. Click-open—Click-close.

Life measured in frames per second
And moments, irreconcilable in time.
Invisible bullets snapping air overhead.
Pockmarked scars on buildings are reflections.

The shutter finger presses closed an artery
That paints eyes in blinding crimson—click-open.
Screaming light pours in, begging for the sound ...
All is quiet in a blown exposure.

Disquieted eyes track blood trails behind
Toward a sun-swallowed silhouette, wandering
Dazed in the distance, where colors bleed
Across the horizon. The shutter clicks again, and

Returning Soldiers Speak

Shadows are all that remain.
The lost and formless frames of war,
The painful echoes of the voiceless—
There are no explanations in these images.

32

Intravenous
by Hugh Martin

A rope of black smoke
above the city. Police sirens. The feet
of the crowd over pavement.
We don't know who she is: barely

a year alive, her blue leggings wet, stuck
to the skin with her own blood.
Doc Johnson holds her head
like an orange in his open hand. He kneels

beside the white Opel while Kenson aims
the mounted light from his M4
through the shattered window to her face,
the glass spread around her

like rock salt on the brown
seat cushions. Doc scissors her cotton sleeve,
pushes his thumb to her arm for a vein—nothing…
He finds one, eye to hairline, pulsing

with her screams; he wipes the skin
with antiseptic, and with one hand,
steadies her head as an Imam's voice
blankets the night in waves; cars filled

with wounded weave around us with the dust.
Doc lowers the needle to this girl's blue vein,
and it touches her skin like pricking
the Tigris on a smooth map of the earth.

waiting to say amen

About the Authors

R. S. Carlson, a professor of English at Azusa Pacific University, Azusa, CA., was an Army Specialist 5th Class at the 8th Radio Research Field Station, Phu Bai, and the 407th Radio Research Detachment, Quang Tri Province, Viet Nam, 1970-1971, serving as a Vietnamese language Voice Intercept Operator and Translator/Interpreter. Ralph has published over 440 poems in print and online journals, including Poetry/LA; Northwest Review; The Texas Review; Poet Lore; The Hawai'i Review; War, Literature and the Arts; Viet Nam Generation; Sunstone; The Panhandler, The Listening Eye, and Praesidium. His book "Waiting to Say Amen" was published in 2010.

Gary Champagne is from The Turtle Mountain Indian Reservation and is a member of The Pembina Band of Chippewa. He served in the Air Force as an Air Traffic Controller at McClellan AFB from 1979-80. A graduate of California State University Stanislaus with a BA in English, he began experimenting in creative writing in the spring of 2013. *Slam It Baby* is a true story with the names and place omitted to protect the innocent.

Amy Feemster served in the US Navy, as a cryptologic technician maintenance (CTM) during the years 1986-1989. Amy was honorably discharged for pregnancy with her first daughter. The poem "The Uniform" was written about the decision to end her career with the Navy and follow her maternal instincts. She is a creative person and was born July 23, 1965, in the state of California to a working dad and stay at home mom. She has four grown children who create beyond her expectations and are a great filling of light in her life. She has published one book entitled "Snowfield Autumn", a collection of prose. Art and writing help her to express where vocalization takes a turn to impact in a loud perfunctory statement that sometimes rankles. She resides in Los Angeles, California.

Sonny Fox was born in Brooklyn on June 17, 1925, young Irwin (his given and rarely used name) toughed out the Depression. His college career at NYU was interrupted by World War II and was a sergeant in the 28th infantry division. Fox was captured by the Germans in the Battle of the Bulge and ended up in the only German POW camp that separated the Jewish GIs from the others. Saved from a slave labor camp by an improbable intervention, Fox narrated the latest war news from a secret radio to his fellow POWs and organized speaking programs in the barracks. After the war he graduated with a degree in Radio Production from NYU. He joined the Voice of America in 1950 as a correspondent and in 1952 began a yearlong tour as its war correspondent in Korea. From 1959 to 1967 on "Wonderama," Fox entertained and enlightened New York area kids for four hours every Sunday. Dressed in a suit and tie, and loathe to treat his in-studio and viewing audiences as anything less than unique human beings, Fox built a bond of trust between him and his audience that has rarely, if ever, been matched. He lives in Encino with his "late in life gift," Celestine Arndt.

William Galloway, Army Alpha CO 603rd Battalion, 2005-2007; *Returning Soldiers Speak* Facebook Page Administrator. He believes in equality and peace but understands that real freedoms have to be fought for. He uses his words to help with that battle. He believes that we, together, working towards one goal cannot be stopped...

Dick Howell is a veteran of the USAF, 1960-1963, where he completed an undistinguished enlistment as a clerk typist at Davis Monthan Air Force Base in Tucson. Dick has taught high school, drove trucks and worked as a union pipefitter and an oil patch roughneck. He has run two motorcycle clubs, drove racecars and served two terms as student body president while getting his AA and BA from Cuesta Junior College and Cal Poly University. He lives in Santa Maria, California.

Ken Klemm is a veteran of the United States Navy, and Budweiser, Miller, Coors and whatever else was in front of him at the time. He is a 46-year old alcoholic writer, which may be redundant. He obtained help and achieved sobriety through the Veteran Administration's Domiciliary Program, a residential treatment facility in West Los Angeles. He is getting back into the craft of writing after a 30-year journey through the world of the bottle. He now looks forward to putting pen to paper instead of fleeing from it. He is currently moving forward with his life, moving from homelessness to housing and employment. He lives in Los Angeles with no wife, kids, or dogs.

Hugh Martin is a veteran of the Iraq war and the author of *The Stick Soldiers* (BOA Editions, Ltd., 2013) and *So, How Was the War* (Kent State UP, 2010). His work has appeared recently in *The Kenyon Review*, *The New Republic*, and *The New York Times'* At War blog. Martin has an MFA from Arizona State and he is currently a Stegner Fellow at Stanford University.

James Mathers, USN 1954-56. USAF 1956-58. Mathers began his career in the 60's in Hollywood, writing low-budget features and TV episodics including *Sabbat* and *Death Valley Days*. In the 70's his work focused on working as actor and playwright in San Francisco at the Magic Theater and others, where credits include *Desire Under the Elms* and *The Right Stuff*. New York credits include *Happy Birthday Wanda June* and *Lion in Winter*. Hollywood again for the new millenia with features, TV, copious cable, internet, and new media. An oldie but goodie who spends his time writing, acting, developing new material at the Studio City Writers Group and herding cats. Catch him most recently on *Ray Donovan*. Find Mathers' reel, pictures and resume at www.imbd.com, pitching at www.studio44hollywood.com, and www.studiocitywritersgroup.com

Terry Mickel was born and raised in Mississippi, a country boy. He joined the army at 17 and left home to begin his military obligation fresh out of high school. He was assigned to the 101st Airborne Unit during the Gulf War. He was awarded two Bronze Stars for actions in the conflict. He enjoys writing and looks forward to "A Soldier's Tale," being published in the *Returning Soldiers Speak* anthology. He enjoys doing a lot of different things like acting, directing, playing sports. Writing however puts him in an entirely different state of mind that's focused and peaceful.

James F. Miller was a LT Commander in the Navy's SEAL TEAM 2. He did three tours in Vietnam from 1967-1973 where he spent more time in Cambodia than Vietnam working for the CIA. He received Silver Star and Bronze Stars and the reason he was awarded them is between him and the dead he could not save. Jim was a wide receiver for the Houston Oilers from 1968-71. "My First Christmas in Vietnam," won Second Place in the category of a personal experience, patriotic, in the 2011 Department of Veterans Affairs, National Veterans Creative Arts Competition.

John Rixey Moore entered the U.S. Army as a buck private just after college, and got out a few months under four years later as a Sergeant First Class, E-7. John served in the Special Forces (Green Berets) and was also an Airborne Ranger. John's decorations include The Distinguished Service Cross, 2 Silver Stars, 5 Bronze Stars, 3 Purple Hearts, the Vietnamese Cross of Gallantry-First Order, and five to six additional conduct and unit service citations. John has written a memoir of his Vietnam experience in a book titled *Hostage of Paradox: A Qualmish Disclosure* published in 2012 by Bettie Youngs Book Publishers. To date, the book has been translated into Chinese Foreign Rights, and has received a number of awards, including being a Pulitzer Prize entry; the Colby prize for Best Military Book of the Year; and the 2012 USA Best Book of the Year Finalist. John's second book, a sequel to Hostage of Paradox, is titled "Company of Stone: A Memoir" and was published in 2013 (Bettie Youngs Book Publishers). Both books are available online at *Amazon* and *Barnes & Noble*, and from *Espresso* and *Read How You Want*, and from *Brodart* and *Quality Books*. In addition, Rixey has published a few stories (including the popular *Abucodonozor*— available in ebook online) and poems and has written the "How To" manual on the technique for pushing a bobsled for the US Skeleton and Bobsled Association while he was on the U.S. Bobsled team. Visit his website at www.JohnMoore.com / http://bit.ly/RixeyBlog / http://on.fb.me/POZSS6 Facebook.

Jeffrey Alan Rochlin was drafted in February 1968, and served until February 1970, Medic Specialist 4th Class. He served two years in Germany under United States Army Europe Command and stationed at the 97th General Hospital in Frankfurt, the Medical Headquarters for U. S. Army Europe. He was transferred to the 4th General Dispensary in Darmstadt Germany and spent the remainder of his tour of duty as an Emergency Room Tech. Alan is currently registered as an active member with the Veterans Department. He is a member of ASCAP and a published songwriter. He is a member of Artist Salon working with downtown city council to help develop the downtown artist's community; hosts readings at Stories Book Store in Echo Park and various venues around Los Angeles; Guest Host at "100,000 Thousand Poets for Change" at Beyond Baroque; Director of Valley Contemporary Poets for the past 5 years; and works with Richard Modiano doing promotion and volunteer work at Beyond Baroque Literary Arts Center in Venice, California.

Ethan E. Rocke served as a combat correspondent in the Marine Corps from 2001 to 2011 and in the Army as an infantryman from 1998 to 2001, during which time he served in Kosovo. He is a professional storyteller and award-winning writer and photojournalist. He writes pretty words with passion, makes pictures with poignancy, and is a budding DSLR filmmaker, striving to be a genuine world shaker—a bonafide fourth-estater and all-out Truth crusader. He holds a BS in Photojournalism from Syracuse University and will complete his MS in Multimedia Journalism from the University of Oregon in December 2013. View more of his work at http://www.ethanrocke. com.

Michael Sadler was a Navy hospital corpsman in Da Nang, Vietnam during 1969-70, where he received a meritorious field promotion to hospital corpsman 2nd Class (E5). After military service, Michael received his A.S. Degree in BioScience and B.S. Degree in Environmental Studies at U.C. Santa Barbara, and then worked in Washington, D.C. doing energy/environmental research. Returning to California, Michael changed career direction and was a general building contractor for almost 20 years. Michael retired and started writing novels (3 published), stage plays (2 dozen produced works), and a short subject screenplay, winning top honors in 2009 in 3 national screenwriting competitions.

Earl Smallwood, Jr. was born on November 23, 1947 in Hogansville, Georgia. He served in the U. S. Army from 1968 to 1971, and was stationed at Ft. Benning, Georgia, 1968; Ft. Leonard Wood, Missouri, 1968; Long Bien, Vietnam, 1968-69; and Ft. Rucker, Alabama, 1969-71. He attended West Georgia College, earning a BBA in Management in 1976. Earl earned his Georgia Real Estate License in 1991. Married twice, Earl has two children, two stepchildren and five grandchildren. He has worked in various management positions for many companies for over 30 years. His hobbies are fishing, scuba diving, gardening, and chasing ground squirrels from his backyard with his BB gun. Current Status: wonderfully retired.

Jim Terpstra, U.S. Navy, 1987-1994, does not like to blow his own horn. His modesty can be contributed to his self-effacing attitude and an uncontrollable need to blush at the drop of a hat. Any accolades make him sprint the other way. Like high school and his military training, Jim graduated college believing they must have made a huge mistake by either getting his name mixed up with someone else or he bribed someone without remembering. He only wants to make as many people laugh as possible so sitcom writing is what he is pursuing.

Burk Wiedner was born in 1935 in Berlin. He and his family survived the war but after Germany's capitulation, their home lay a mere eighty yards outside city limits in what would shortly become Russian-controlled East

Germany. Burk left home and family three days after his 18th birthday. He applied for political asylum and worked in a variety of jobs in the "West," until his acceptance at the College of Political Science in West Berlin. In early 1955, he received his visa and immigrated to Santa Barbara, California. Entering the Army a year later, he served in Butzbach, Germany. Following his discharge Burk worked himself through undergraduate studies and law school. He retired from corporate law practice in 2002, and lives with his wife Gail in Santa Clarita, California.

About Leilani Squire

Leilani Squire is a writer, screenwriting consultant and CCA Certified Creativity Coach. Her father served thirty years in the Navy so she has an insider's view of military life. She facilitates weekly creative writing workshops at the West Los Angeles Veterans Hospital and Wellness Works, Glendale. James F. Miller, one of her students, placed 2nd in the Patriotic Essay category for the 2011 Department of Veterans Affairs National Veterans Creative Arts Festival and gave her his silver medal, which is one of the highest honors she has ever received. Visit www.returningsoldiersspeak.org and Like on Facebook at www.facebook.com/ReturningSoldiersSpeak

Other Books by Bettie Youngs Book Publishers

Hostage of Paradox: *A Qualmish Disclosure*

John Rixey Moore

Few people then or now know about the clandestine war that the CIA ran in Vietnam, using the Green Berets for secret operations throughout Southeast Asia. This was not the Vietnam War of the newsreels, the body counts, rice paddy footage, and men smoking cigarettes on the sandbag bunkers. This was a shadow directive of deep-penetration interdiction, reconnaissance, and assassination missions conducted by a selected few Special Forces units, deployed quietly from forward operations bases to prowl through agendas that, for security reasons, were seldom understood by the men themselves.

Hostage of Paradox is the first-hand account by one of these elite team leaders.

"Deserving of a place in the upper ranks of Vietnam War memoirs." —**Kirkus Review**

"Read this book, you'll be, as John Moore puts it, 'transfixed, like kittens in a box.'" —**David Willson, Book Review, The VVA Veteran**

ISBN: 978-1-936332-37-3 • ePub: 978-1-936332-33-5

Company of Stone

John Rixey Moore

With yet unhealed wounds from recent combat, John Moore undertook an unexpected walking tour in the rugged Scottish highlands. With the approach of a season of freezing rainstorms he took shelter in a remote monastery—a chance encounter that would change his future, his beliefs about blind chance, and the unexpected courses by which the best in human nature can smuggle its way into the life of a stranger. Afterwards, a chance conversation overheard in a village pub steered him to Canada, where he took a job as a rock drill operator in a large industrial gold mine. The dangers he encountered among the lost men in that dangerous other world, secretive men who sought permanent anonymity in the perils of work deep underground—a brutal kind of monasticism itself—challenged both his endurance and his sense of humanity.

With sensitivity and delightful good humor, Moore explores the surprising lessons learned in these strangely rich fraternities of forgotten men—a brotherhood housed in crumbling medieval masonry, and one shared in the unforgiving depths of the gold mine.

ISBN: 978-1-936332-44-1 • ePub: 978-1-936332-45-8

Last Reader Standing
... The Story of a Man Who Learned to Read at 54

Archie Willard
with Colleen Wiemerslage

The day Archie lost his thirty-one year job as a laborer at a meat packing company, he was forced to confront the secret he had held so closely for most of his life: at the age of fifty-four, he couldn't read. For all his adult life, he'd been able to skirt around the issue. But now, forced to find a new job to support his family, he could no longer hide from the truth.

Last Reader Standing is the story of Archie's amazing—and often painful—journey of becoming literate at middle age, struggling with the newfound knowledge of his dyslexia. From the little boy who was banished to the back of the classroom because the teachers labeled him "stupid," Archie emerged to becoming a national figure who continues to enlighten professionals into the world of the learning disabled. He joined Barbara Bush on stage for her Literacy Foundation's fundraisers where she proudly introduced him as "the man who took advantage of a second chance and improved his life."

This is a touching and poignant story that gives us an eye-opening view of the lack of literacy in our society, and how important it is for all of us to have opportunity to become all that we can be—to have hope and go after our dreams.

At the age of eighty-two, Archie continues to work with literacy issues in medicine and consumerism.

"Archie . . . you need to continue spreading the word." —**Barbara Bush, founder of the Literacy Foundation, and First Lady and wife of George H. W. Bush, the 41st President of the United States**

ISBN: 978-1-936332-48-9 • ePub: 978-1-936332-50-2

Fastest Man in the World
The Tony Volpentest Story

Tony Volpentest
Foreword by Ross Perot

Tony Volpentest, a four-time Paralympic gold medalist and five-time world champion sprinter, is a 2012 nominee for the Olympic Hall of Fame. This inspirational story details his being born without feet, to holding records as the fastest sprinter in the world.

"This inspiring story is about the thrill of victory to be sure—winning gold—but it is also a reminder about human potential: the willingness to push ourselves beyond the ledge of our own imagination. A powerfully inspirational story." —**Charlie Huebner, United States Olympic Committee**

ISBN: 978-1-936332-00-7 • ePub: 978-1-936332-01-4

The Maybelline Story
And the Spirited Family Dynasty Behind It

Sharrie Williams

A fascinating and inspiring story, a tale both epic and intimate, alive with the clash, the hustle, the music, and dance of American enterprise.

"A richly told story of a forty-year, white-hot love triangle that fans the flames of a major worldwide conglomerate." —**Neil Shulman, Associate Producer,** *Doc Hollywood*

"Salacious! Engrossing! There are certain stories so dramatic, so sordid, that they seem positively destined for film; this is one of them." —*New York Post*

ISBN: 978-0-9843081-1-8 • ePub: 978-1-936332-17-5

On Toby's Terms

Charmaine Hammond

On Toby's Terms is an endearing story of a beguiling creature who teaches his owners that, despite their trying to teach him how to be the dog they want, he is the one to lay out the terms of being the dog he needs to be. This insight would change their lives forever.

"This is a captivating, heartwarming story and we are very excited about bringing it to film." —**Steve Hudis, Producer**

ISBN: 978-0-9843081-4-9 • ePub: 978-1-936332-15-1

Blackbird Singing in the Dead of Night
What to Do When God Won't Answer

Updated Edition with Study Guide

Gregory L. Hunt

Pastor Greg Hunt had devoted nearly thirty years to congregational ministry, helping people experience God and find their way in life. Then came his own crisis of faith and calling. While turning to God for guidance, he finds nothing. Neither his education nor his religious involvements could prepare him for the disorienting impact of the experience. Alarmed, he tries an experiment. The result is startling—and changes his life entirely.

"Compelling. If you have ever longed to hear God whispering a love song into your life, read this book." —**Gary Chapman,** *NY Times* **bestselling author,** *The Love Languages of God*

ISBN: 978-0-9882848-9-0 • ePub: 978-1-936332-52-6

The Rebirth of Suzzan Blac

Suzzan Blac

A horrific upbringing and then abduction into the sex slave industry would all but kill Suzzan's spirit to live. But a happy marriage and two children brought love—and forty-two stunning paintings, art so raw that it initially frightened even the artist. "I hid the pieces for 15 years," says Suzzan, "but just as with the secrets in this book, I am slowing sneaking them out, one by one by one." Now a renowned artist, her work is exhibited world-wide. A story of inspiration, truth and victory.

"A solid memoir about a life reconstructed. Chilling, thrilling, and thought provoking."
—**Pearry Teo, Producer,** *The Gene Generation*

ISBN: 978-1-936332-22-9 • ePub: 978-1-936332-23-6

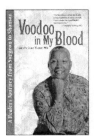

Voodoo in My Blood
A Healer's Journey from Surgeon to Shaman

Carolle Jean-Murat, M.D.

Born and raised in Haiti to a family of healers, US trained physician Carolle Jean-Murat came to be regarded as a world-class surgeon. But her success harbored a secret: in the operating room, she could quickly intuit the root cause of her patient's illness, often times knowing she could help the patient without surgery. Carolle knew that to fellow surgeons, her intuition was best left unmentioned. But when the devastating earthquake hit Haiti and Carolle returned to help, she had to acknowledge the shaman she had become.

"This fascinating memoir sheds light on the importance of asking yourself, 'Have I created for myself the life I've meant to live?'" —**Christiane Northrup, M.D., author of the New York Times bestsellers:** *Women's Bodies, Women's Wisdom*

ISBN: 978-1-936332-05-2 • ePub: 978-1-936332-04-5

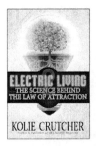

Electric Living
The Science behind the Law of Attraction

Kolie Crutcher

An electrical engineer by training, Crutcher applies his in-depth knowledge of electrical engineering principles and practical engineering experience detailing the scientific explanation of why human beings become what they think. A practical, step-by-step guide to help you harness your thoughts and emotions so that the Law of Attraction will benefit you.

ISBN: 978-1-936332-58-8 • ePub: 978-1-936332-59-5

DON CARINA: *WWII Mafia Heroine*

Ron Russell

A father's death in Southern Italy in the 1930s—a place where women who can read are considered unfit for marriage—thrusts seventeen-year-old Carina into servitude as a "black widow," a legal head of the household who cares for her twelve siblings. A scandal forces her into a marriage to Russo, the "Prince of Naples." By cunning force, Carina seizes control of Russo's organization and disguising herself as a man, controls the most powerful of Mafia groups for nearly a decade.

"A woman as the head of the Mafia who shows her family her resourcefulness, strength and survival techniques. Unique, creative and powerful! This exciting book blends history, intrigue and power into one delicious epic adventure that you will not want to put down!" —**Linda Gray, Actress,** *Dallas*

ISBN: 978-0-9843081-9-4 • ePub: 978-1-936332-49-6

Amazing Adventures of a Nobody

Leon Logothetis

From the Hit Television Series Aired in 100 Countries!

Tired of his disconnected life and uninspiring job, Leon Logothetis leaves it all behind—job, money, home, even his cell phone—and hits the road with nothing but the clothes on his back and five dollars in his pocket, relying on the kindness of strangers and the serendipity of the open road for his daily keep. Masterful storytelling!

"A gem of a book; endearing, engaging and inspiring." —**Catharine Hamm, Los Angeles Times Travel Editor**

ISBN: 978-0-9843081-3-2 • ePub: 978-1-936332-51-9

MR. JOE
Tales from a Haunted Life

Joseph Barnett and Jane Congdon

Do you believe in ghosts? Joseph Barnett didn't, until the winter he was fired from his career job and became a school custodian. Assigned the graveyard shift, Joe was confronted with a series of bizarre and terrifying occurrences.

"Thrilling, thoughtful, elegantly told. So much more than a ghost story." —**Cyrus Webb, CEO, Conversation Book Club**

ISBN: 978-1-936332-78-6 • ePub: 978-1-936332-79-3

Out of the Transylvania Night

Aura Imbarus
A Pulitzer-Prize entry

"I'd grown up in the land of Transylvania, homeland to Dracula, Vlad the Impaler, and worse, dictator Nicolae Ceausescu," writes the author. "Under his rule, like vampires, we came to life after sundown, hiding our heirloom jewels and documents deep in the earth." Fleeing to the US to rebuild her life, she discovers a startling truth about straddling two cultures and striking a balance between one's dreams and the sacrifices that allow a sense of "home."

"Aura's courage shows the degree to which we are all willing to live lives centered on freedom, hope, and an authentic sense of self. Truly a love story!" —**Nadia Comaneci, Olympic Champion**

ISBN: 978-0-9843081-2-5 • ePub: 978-1-936332-20-5

Living with Multiple Personalities
The Christine Ducommun Story

Christine Ducommun

Christine Ducommun was a happily married wife and mother of two, when—after moving back into her childhood home—she began to experience panic attacks and bizarre flashbacks. Eventually diagnosed with Dissociative Identity Disorder (DID), Christine's story details an extraordinary twelve-year ordeal unraveling the buried trauma of her forgotten past.

"Reminiscent of the Academy Award-winning *A Beautiful Mind,* this true story will have you on the edge of your seat. Spellbinding!" —**Josh Miller, Producer**

ISBN: 978-0-9843081-5-6 • ePub: 978-1-936332-06-9

The Tortoise Shell Code

V Frank Asaro

Off the coast of Southern California, the Sea Diva, a tuna boat, sinks. Members of the crew are missing and what happened remains a mystery. Anthony Darren, a renowned and wealthy lawyer at the top of his game, knows the boat's owner and soon becomes involved in the case. As the case goes to trial, a missing crew member is believed to be at fault, but new evidence comes to light and the finger of guilt points in a completely unanticipated direction. An action-packed thriller.

ISBN: 978-1-936332-60-1 • ePub: 978-1-936332-61-8

The Search for the Lost Army
The National Geographic and
Harvard University Expedition

Gary S. Chafetz

In one of history's greatest ancient disasters, a Persian army of 50,000 soldiers was suffocated by a hurricane-force sandstorm in 525 BC in Egypt's Western Desert. No trace of this conquering army, hauling huge quantities of looted gold and silver, has ever surfaced.

Gary Chafetz, referred to as "one of the ten best journalists of the past twenty-five years," is a former Boston Globe correspondent and was twice nominated for a Pulitzer Prize by the Globe.

ISBN: 978-1-936332-98-4 • ePub: 978-1-936332-99-1

A World Torn Asunder
The Life and Triumph of Constantin C. Giurescu

Marina Giurescu, M.D.

Constantin C. Giurescu was Romania's leading historian and author. His granddaughter's fascinating story of this remarkable man and his family follows their struggles in war-torn Romania from 1900 to the fall of the Soviet Union. An "enlightened" society is dismantled with the 1946 Communist takeover of Romania, and Constantin is confined to the notorious Sighet penitentiary. Drawing on her grandfather's prison diary (which was put in a glass jar, buried in a yard, then smuggled out of the country by Dr. Paul E. Michelson—who does the FOREWORD for this book), private letters and her own research, Dr. Giurescu writes of the legacy from the turn of the century to the fall of Communism.

We see the rise of modern Romania, the misery of World War I, the blossoming of its culture between the wars, and then the sellout of Eastern Europe to Russia after World War II. In this sweeping account, we see not only its effects socially and culturally, but the triumph in its wake: a man and his people who reclaim better lives for themselves, and in the process, teach us a lesson in endurance, patience, and will—not only to survive, but to thrive.

"The inspirational story of a quiet man and his silent defiance in the face of tyranny."
—**Dr. Connie Mariano, author of** *The White House Doctor*

ISBN: 978-1-936332-76-2 • ePub: 978-1-936332-77-9

Diary of a Beverly Hills Matchmaker

Marla Martenson

Quick-witted Marla takes her readers for a hilarious romp through her days as an LA matchmaker where looks are everything and money talks. The Cupid of Beverly Hills has introduced countless couples who lived happily ever-after, but for every success story there are hysterically funny dating disasters with high-maintenance, out of touch clients. Marla writes with charm and self-effacement about the universal struggle to love and be loved.

ISBN 978-0-9843081-0-1 • ePub: 978-1-936332-03-8

The Morphine Dream

Don Brown with Pulitzer nominated Gary S. Chafetz

At 36, high-school dropout and a failed semi-professional ballplayer Donald Brown hit bottom when an industrial accident left him immobilized. But Brown had a dream while on a morphine drip after surgery: he imagined himself graduating from Harvard Law School (he was a classmate of Barack Obama) and walking across America. Brown realizes both seemingly unreachable goals, and achieves national recognition as a legal crusader for minority homeowners. An intriguing tale of his long walk—both physical and metaphorical. A story of perseverance and second chances. Sheer inspiration for those wishing to reboot their lives.

"An incredibly inspirational memoir." —**Alan M. Dershowitz, professor, Harvard Law School**

ISBN: 978-1-936332-25-0 • ePub: 978-1-936332-39-7

The Girl Who Gave Her Wish Away

Sharon Babineau
Foreword by Craig Kielburger

The Children's Wish Foundation approached lovely thirteen-year-old Maddison Babineau just after she received her cancer diagnosis. "You can have anything," they told her, "a Disney cruise? The chance to meet your favorite movie star? A five thousand dollar shopping spree?"

Maddie knew exactly what she wanted. She had recently been moved to tears after watching a television program about the plight of orphaned children. Maddie's wish? To ease the suffering of these children half-way across the world. Despite the ravishing cancer, she became an indefatigable fundraiser for "her children." In The Girl Who Gave Wish Away, her mother reveals Maddie's remarkable journey of providing hope and future to the village children who had filled her heart.

A special story, heartwarming and reassuring.

ISBN: 978-1-936332-96-0 • ePub: 978-1-936332-97-7

The Ten Commandments for Travelers

Nancy Chappie

Traveling can be an overwhelming experience fraught with delays, tension, and unexpected complications. But whether you're traveling for business or pleasure, alone or with family or friends, there are things you can do to make your travels more enjoyable—even during the most challenging experiences. Easy to implement tips for hassle-free travel, and guidance for those moments that threaten to turn your voyage into an unpleasant experience. You'll learn how to avoid extra costs and aggravations, save time, and stay safe; how to keep your cool under the worst of circumstances, how to embrace new cultures, and how to fully enjoy each moment you're on the road.

ISBN: 978-1-936332-74-8 • ePub: 978-1-936332-75-5

GPS YOUR BEST LIFE
Charting Your Destination and Getting There in Style

Charmaine Hammond and Debra Kasowski
Foreword by Jack Canfield

A most useful guide to charting and traversing the many options that lay before you.

"A perfect book for servicing your most important vehicle: yourself. No matter where you are in your life, the concepts and direction provided in this book will help you get to a better place. It's a must read." —**Ken Kragen, author of** *Life Is a Contact Sport*, **and organizer of** *We Are the World*, **and** *Hands Across America*, **and other historic humanitarian events**

ISBN: 978-1-936332-26-7 • ePub: 978-1-936332-41-0

Crashers
A Tale of "Cappers" and "Hammers"

Lindy S. Hudis

The illegal business of fraudulent car accidents is a multi-million dollar racket, involving unscrupulous medical providers, personal injury attorneys, and the cooperating passengers involved in the accidents. Innocent people are often swept into it. Newly engaged Nathan and Shari, who are swimming in mounting debt, were easy prey: seduced by an offer from a stranger to move from hard times to good times in no time, Shari finds herself the "victim" in a staged auto accident. Shari gets her payday, but breaking free of this dark underworld will take nothing short of a miracle.

"A riveting story of love, life—and limits. A non-stop thrill ride." —**Dennis "Danger" Madalone, stunt coordinator,** *Castle*

ISBN: 978-1-936332-27-4 • ePub: 978-1-936332-28-1

Thank You for Leaving Me
Finding Divinity and Healing in Divorce

Farhana Dhalla
Foreword by Neale Donald Walsch

The end of any relationship, especially divorce, can leave us bereft, feeling unmoored, empty. Speaking to that part of our hearts that knows you must find your way to a new and different place, this compassionate book of words of wisdom helps grow this glimmering knowledge—and offers hope and healing for turning this painful time into one of renewal and rediscovery. This book is balm for your wounded heart, and can help you turn your fragility to endurable coping, and will you rediscover your inner strengths. Best of all, this book will help you realize the transformative power inherent in this transition.

ISBN: 978-1-936332-85-4 • ePub: 978-1-936332-86-1

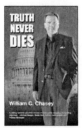

Truth Never Dies

William C. Chasey

A lobbyist for some 40 years, William C. Chasey represented some of the world's most prestigious business clients and twenty-three foreign governments before the US Congress. His integrity never questioned. All that changed when Chasey was hired to forge communications between Libya and the US Congress. A trip he took with a US Congressman for discussions with then Libyan leader Muammar Qadhafi forever changed Chasey's life. Upon his return, his bank accounts were frozen, clients and friends had been advised not to take his calls.

Things got worse: the CIA, FBI, IRS, and the Federal Judiciary attempted to coerce him into using his unique Libyan access to participate in a CIA-sponsored assassination plot of the two Libyans indicted for the bombing of Pan Am flight 103. Chasey's refusal to cooperate resulted in a six-year FBI investigation and sting operation, financial ruin, criminal charges, and incarceration in federal prison.

ISBN: 978-1-936332-46-5 • ePub: 978-1-936332-47-2

Trafficking the Good Life

Jennifer Myers

Jennifer Myers had worked hard toward a successful career as a dancer in Chicago. But just as her star was rising, she fell for the kingpin of a drug trafficking operation. Drawn to his life of excitement, she soon acquiesced to driving marijuana across the country, making easy money she stacked in shoeboxes and spent like an heiress. Only time in a federal prison made her face up to and understand her choices. It was there, at rock bottom, that she discovered that her real prison was the one she had unwittingly made inside herself and where she could start rebuilding a life of purpose and ethical pursuit.

"In her gripping memoir Jennifer Myers offers a startling account of how the pursuit of an elusive American Dream can lead us to the depths of the American criminal underbelly. Her book is as much about being human in a hyper-materialistic society as it is about drug culture. When the DEA finally knocks on Myers' door, she and the reader both see the moment for what it truly is—not so much an arrest as a rescue." —**Tony D'Souza, author of** ***Whiteman and Mule***

ISBN: 978-1-936332-67-0 • ePub: 978-1-936332-68-7

Universal Co-opetition
Nature's Fusion of Co-operation and Competition

V Frank Asaro

A key ingredient in personal and business success is competition—and cooperation. Too much of one or the other can erode personal and organizational goals. This book identifies and explains the natural, fundamental law that unifies the apparently opposing forces of cooperation and competition.

ISBN: 978-1-936332-08-3 • ePub: 978-1-936332-09-0

Cinderella and the Carpetbagger

Grace Robbins

Harold Robbins's steamy books were once more widely read than the Bible. His novels sold more than 750 million copies and created the sex-power-glamour genre of popular literature that would go on to influence authors from Jackie Collins and Jacqueline Susann to TV shows like Dallas and Dynasty. What readers don't know is that Robbins—whom the media had dubbed the "prince of sex and scandal"—actually "researched" the free-wheeling escapades depicted in his books himself . . . along with his drop-dead, gorgeous wife, Grace. Now, in this revealing tell-all, for the first time ever, Grace Robbins rips the covers off the real life of the international best-selling author.

The 1960s and '70s were decades like no others—radical, experimental, libertine. Grace Robbins chronicles the rollicking good times, peppering her memoir with anecdotes of her encounters with luminaries from the world of entertainment and the arts—not to mention most of Hollywood. The couple was at the center of a globetrotting jet set, with mansions in Beverly Hills, villas and yachts on the French Riviera and Acapulco. Their life rivaled—and often surpassed—that of the characters in his books. Champagne flowed, cocaine was abundant, and sex in the pre-AIDS era was embraced with abandon. Along the way, the couple agreed to a "modern marriage," that Harold insisted upon. With charm, introspection, and humor, Grace lays open her fascinating, provocative roller-coaster ride of a life—her own true Cinderella tale.

"This sweet little memoir's getting a movie deal." —**New York Post**

"I gulped down every juicy minute of this funny, outrageous memoir. Do not take a pill before you go to bed with this book, because you will not be able to put it down until the sun comes up." —**Rex Reed**

"Grace Robbins has written an explosive tell-all. Sexy fun." —**Jackie Collins**

"You have been warned. This book is VERY HOT!" —**Robin Leach, Lifestyles of the Rich & Famous**

ISBN: 978-0-9882848-2-1 • ePub: 978-0-9882848-4-5

It Started with Dracula
The Count, My Mother, and Me

Jane Congdon

The terrifying legend of Count Dracula silently skulking through the Transylvania night may have terrified generations of filmgoers, but the tall, elegant vampire captivated and electrified a young Jane Congdon, igniting a dream to one day see his mysterious land of ancient castles and misty hollows. Four decades later she finally takes her long-awaited trip—never dreaming that it would unearth decades-buried memories, and trigger a life-changing inner journey. A memoir full of surprises, Jane's story is one of hope, love—and second chances.

"An elegantly written and cleverly told story. An electrifying read." —**Diane Bruno, CISION Media**

ISBN: 978-1-936332-10-6 • ePub: 978-1-936332-11-3

Bettie Youngs Books

We specialize in MEMOIRS

. . . books that celebrate

fascinating people and

remarkable journeys

If you are unable to order this book from your local
bookseller, or online from Amazon or Barnes & Noble,
or from Espresso or Read How You Want,
you may order directly from the publisher
at info@BettieYoungsBooks.com.

VISIT OUR WEBSITE AT
www.BettieYoungsBooks.com

CPSIA information can be obtained at www.ICGtesting.com
Printed in the USA
LVOW12s0708101013

356281LV00003B/7/P

9 781936 332625